MW00620395

THE ULTIMATE FLIGHT

THE ULTIMATE FLIGHT

IN SEARCH OF MIKE

Martha Gunsalus Chamberlain

Wesley Press
Indianapolis, Indiana

Cover photograph of Mike Mueller flying an A-4 jet by Bill Jeffries.

Design and typesetting by Denise Mueller Eash.

Second printing

Published by Wesley Press
Indianapolis, Indiana 46250
Printed in the United States of America
ISBN: 0-89827-186-X
Library of Congress Catalog Card Number: 96-60728

ACKNOWLEDGMENTS

Attribution for excerpts from newspapers are included in the text and are quoted by permission from: *The Chronicle Tribune*, Marion, Indiana, May 27, 1987, Steve Griffith; *Times-Delta*, Visalia, California, May 27, 1987, Steve Griffith; *The News Journal*, Pensacola, Florida, April 18, 1988, Elizabeth Donovan; *the sun*, Tempe, Arizona, June 4, 1987, Katrina Stonoff; *The Washington Post*, Washington, D.C., November 21, 1987, Molly Moore; the *Examiner-Enterprise*, Bartlesville, Oklahoma, April 14, 1989; The United Media Enterprises (Syndicate), New York City, Jack Anderson and Dale Van Atta's column appearing (nationwide) Sunday, April 14, 1988; the San Jose *Mercury News*, July 17, 1989, by Steve Johnson.

Quotations from the following are used by permission: "Children" from *The Prophet*, by Kahlil Gibran, copyright 1983, Alfred A. Knopf, New York; *The Wind Beneath My Wings*, by Larry Henley and Jeff Silbar, (C) 1982 Warner House of Music & WB Gold Music Corp. WARNER BROS. PUBLICATIONS U.S. INC., Miami, FL 33014. "Seeing the Holy in the Ordinary" by Macrina Wiederkehr, *A Tree Full of Angels*, copyright 1994. Utilizing a Library of Congress copyright search, attempts to contact Bessie Carol Hicks for permission to print her poem, *He Had Wings*, were unsuccessful. It is printed with gratitude to the author. Scripture quotations are taken from *The Holy Bible: New International Version*, (NIV) unless otherwise noted.

To acknowledge everyone who contributed to writing Mike's story is impossible. More than Mike's story or mine, it belongs to a multitude. Mike's parents, Don and Naomi Mueller of Bartlesville, Oklahoma, cooperatively supported its creation, at times with pain. His sisters, Nadean and Denise, shared time, emotions and information. Lenore Stonoff Swanson graciously provided audiotapes, letters and journals. Marilyn Ginsberg likewise supplied immeasurable research and information. The story could not have been written without their support and assistance. Denise Mueller

Eash provided expertise in typesetting and design; Mary Ann Garnett patiently answered all questions about publishing.

Mike's personal friends are legion; they lived the story before I wrote it. Among them these granted interviews and shared memories, letters, journals, poetry, essays and audiotapes: Alan Chamberlain, Eugene Snyman, Lance Carr, Mary Ruth Brown, Ken Hada, Terry Hughes, Ginny Krenning, Phil and Edna Ekstrom, Gerald Ireland, Vic Jones, Jared Bonner, Monte Alexander, Craig and Vilene Horton, Bill Mingle, Scott Slay, Dana Burpo, Esther and Wendell Rovenstine, Mick Rovenstine, E.M. Craighead, Thurlie Tyner, Kevan Mueller, Carlos Kizzie, Bill Jeffries, Tanen, Hurley and Kathy Swartz, John Snook, Jimmy Johnson, Andy and Fran Lockhart, George Ott, Grandma Ireland, Roger Skelley, Alice and Leon Wyatt, Bev Hubbard Hage, Pam Hollman Hofer, Don and Beth Hall, Ron Brown, Diane Kempf, Danny Nelson, Lori and Jo Buck, Alice Ellis, Danny Barron, Cheryl Crouch, Mark Crum, Rick Griffin, Kenneth Satcher, Kevin Montgomery, Carol and Kirk McIntire, Robin and Ray Tetrault and James Tubbs.

Esther Snyman generously opened her home to me for several weeks. Darlene and Don Wilkes provided a retreat in Florida for me to write. Patty and Wes Marquart loaned a car in California and a cabin in the Eastern Sierra to facilitate research and writing during a critical period. The Muellers and Ekstroms helped finance travel and related expenses. Connie McDonald and Betty Pearson offered time and information.

Generous friends at Messiah United Methodist Church in Springfield, Virginia, who provided information and support include: Karen Gardner, MAJ GEN Gary Mears, Rex Wolf, Carl Platt, Nathan Wilkes and Jim Barnett. James Locher gave particularly helpful suggestions for researching/obtaining missing military documents. Noel Widdifield, former military pilot, read the manuscript and assisted with technical aspects and terminology. Robert Gleason (Armed Forces Institute of

Pathology) and Peter Wubbenhorst (Principal Legal Advisor/Special Agent FBI) provided counsel.

The Woolaroc Museum and Bartlesville Chamber of Commerce provided support and information. The U.S. Navy and U.S. Marine Corps helped piece together the story, at times reluctantly and sometimes generously, but all with one stated purpose: to protect national security and the lives of military aviators. Procured military documents as released (JAG/MIR) and quoted, with pseudonyms substituted for implicated personnel, are not classified or copyrighted.

Providing critical information were attorney Richard Brown of San Francisco and Priscilla Lindley, M.D., pathology consultant, who interpreted data. Others giving assistance include: MAJ Paul Waggaman, Lee Vorobyoff, Dennis McGrath, REAR ADM Charles Moore, Bob and Anna Mary Stonoff. Fred Richter, Sally Gaines, David Marquart and Arlene Reveal of the Mono Valley/ Bridgeport area, Lieutenant Terry Padilla and Deputy Randy Hysell of the Bridgeport Sheriff's Department and forest ranger David Marquart each contributed to research and exploration in the Sierra.

Darrell Eash meticulously copyedited the full manuscript. These consultants/readers contributed time and suggestions: Mary Gunsalus, Martha Blackburn, Marcia Chamberlain, the Richmond Readers and Writers group.

With the aid of the following, the manuscript ultimately shrank from 600 to 200 pages—a major miracle. I owe a great debt of gratitude to Russell Chamberlain for his time and expertise in suggesting macro-changes in the manuscript, many of which I followed and others that I ignored—possibly to its detriment. Likewise, Donald R. Gallehr, Alan Cheuse and Terry Zawacki, professors at George Mason University in Fairfax, Virginia, provided editorial assistance during the early developmental stages. Don Brandenburgh, my agent, generously critiqued the full manuscript twice.

Without the pertinent counsel, perpetual encouragement

and ready humor of my dearest companion, Ray Chamberlain, I could not have survived these last nine years. When I finally present him with a published copy, he—above all others—will breathe a sigh of relief.

Finally, I acknowledge God's leadership throughout these nine years of both professional growth and a growing understanding of God at work in all circumstances.

Dedicated

to

Don and Naomi

whose faith is a gift

to us all.

FOREWORD

George Beverly Shea

You may not be able to lay down *The Ultimate Flight* until you have finished the final paragraph. Gifted author Martha Chamberlain paints this fascinating narrative in vivid word pictures.

Mike is an exemplary young man who willingly gave of himself to his country, to his loved ones and friends, and to his Lord and Savior Jesus Christ.

My dear friend, as your eyes and heart take in every word, may you feel the presence of the one who gave himself for you . . . for Mike . . . for all of us who tread the paths and fly the skies in our earthly journey to the ultimate flight.

The anonymous writer of this old song reminds me that our God will one day reveal the hidden secrets and answer our questions. The middle verse reminds us:

If we could know beyond today
As God doth know,
Why dearest treasures pass away
And tears must flow,
And why the darkness leads to light,
Why dreary days will soon grow bright,
Some day life's wrongs will be made right—
Faith tells us so.

CONTENTS

Son of the People,
His laughter nourishes all our tables;
His love burns all our firesides warmer;
His image dots our family albums,
And letters line our book of days.
After God's own heart—
Our son, our brother.

Son of America, Son of Oklahoma,
Our various selves unite in his hard embrace;
He shines in the dark of our discontent
And lifts us soaring to the everlasting sky.
—Mary Ruth Brown
May, 1987

PROLOGUE

Mike was a Marine pilot who flew jets for the Navy. When he disappeared in an F-18 on May 20, 1987, I prayed desperately, hoping he would be found quickly—and alive.

I had grown to love him as a second son. Far from his Oklahoma family, Mike joined our family on weekends and holidays following graduation from the U.S. Naval Academy. He lived God's way in a secular career. But he longed for his orders: Report to flight school.

With a whoop, he celebrated that day. On a spring morning in June, 1985, Mike loaded his belongings onto a flat red trailer he had built for his trip to Pensacola, Florida. At last he was on his way to becoming a pilot. Grinning broadly, he pulled away, taking his passion for flying with him. That passion consumed him.

When I first got the news he had disappeared, I could not have imagined what lay ahead: Christian clairvoyants who insisted Mike was alive; an attorney in San Francisco whose vital clue shocked the family; and even the discovery of Mike's motorcycle key and wallet more than a year later on Kavanaugh Ridge—but not Mike.

Claiming the mystery was solved, the Navy locked its secret files in the Pentagon; Mike's family stopped hiking the Eastern Sierra wilderness to find him; his fiance stored her wedding gown. But, Mike was still missing. We all wanted more than memories, more than pictures. My own love and grief sucked me into the abyss of an obsession: finding Mike.

How and where I found him . . . this is that story.

CHAPTER 1

THE COUNTDOWN

Where can I flee from your presence?
If I go up to the heavens, you are there . . .
If I rise on the wings of the dawn,
If I settle on the far side of the sea,
even there your hand will guide me . . .
—Psalm 139:7-10

At 8:07 A.M. Mike settled into the cockpit. He adjusted his visor and looked into the early morning haze. Sunlight had seeped over the edges of the flat disk that stretched from the Lemoore NAS airfield to the horizon, backlighting the silhouettes of the aircraft lined up on the tarmac. His fingers moved with learned skill and respect for the instrument as though setting the stops of a grandiose pipe organ. In moments he would feel the exhilaration of power flowing through his will, his fingers, his disciplined cognition into the $25 million fighter/attack jet.

The F-18 compelled his respect, but at the same time it waited, passive and useless without the touch of a master. Sometimes Mike forgot the function of the instrument he valued. A surge of power quivered beneath and within him as he taxied to the end of the runway. He quietly thanked God for the glorious day, eager to get on with it.

At 8:38 A.M. small talk ceased. Mike listened to the

omnipresent Air Traffic Control (ATC). Even when silent, ATC looks out for the pilots. Mike understood the language that is Greek to non-fliers: *Cleared to Mina 218/57 via Lemoore 2 departure. Lemoore Hornet 9 routing. Climb and maintain 15 thousand. Expect flight level 200 ten minutes after departure. Squawk 4530*. Issued clearance, Mike fed back to the tower: "Raider 58. Cleared for take-off."

The adrenaline and the fuel mixed. Mike pushed the throttle forward. He surged with the power lift . . . 5, 10, 15 thousand feet out of the reach of all earth-bound creatures plodding the earth beneath him. If anyone looked up at all, they saw only a speck; if they heard any sound, it meant nothing to them. But as Captain Ginsberg and Lieutenant Mueller soared as one with their majestic creature into the magnificent silence on the top side of unbridled freedom, they smiled inside. They all do.

At about ten-minute intervals, three others launched their F-18's into the chain, all with the same mission. Heading north on the prescribed hop, they planned to fly the low-level route from Mono Lake in California to the B-16 target complex at Fallon, Nevada.

9:10. CAPT Ginsberg reported from Raider 58: "Position over Mono Lake at 15,000 VFR. Not visible because of cloud cover."

9:15. Again, he announced: "Heading east or northeast to look for clear weather. Turning radius 55 degree angle of bank. Turn is 2 miles. Speed 360 knots. Altitude 18,000."

9:19. COL Kamp tried to lock in on Raider 58. No response. He inquired about the weather from Raider 60. LT Jordan responded that CAPT Ginsberg went east or northeast to look for a hole.

9:22. LT Jordan communicated from Raider 60: "Locked on an aircraft at 16,000 feet approximately 15-20 nautical miles (NM) northeast of Mono Lake. Is that you, CAPT

Ginsberg? Give me a reading on the weather."

But Raider 58 did not reply. Routine swallowed the minutes. The pilots continued to explore the route. Pilots exercise choice, continually monitoring and assessing the situation with appropriate, measured responses. They agreed to abort the training mission. By ten o'clock Raider 60, Raider 61 and Raider 62 had all headed back to Lemoore NAS.

Their return and landing were uneventful. Beneath their reluctance to admit a serious problem, a nagging awareness rumbled among the pilots like distant thunder. Air Traffic Control continued its attempt to re-establish contact with Raider 58.

10:40. "NAS Lemoore calling Raider 58. CAPT Ginsberg. LT Mueller."

No response.

10:42. "NAS Lemoore calling NAS Fallon. Did Raider 58 land there?"

Discussion followed.

10:50. "ATC NAS Lemoore calling Raider 58. CAPT Ginsberg? LT Mueller?"

Breathing abated, they waited.

*****

Mike Mueller's day had begun at 5:15 A.M. on that Wednesday, May 20, 1987. I wasn't there, but because I knew him and loved him, I can picture him easily. He awoke rested. He laughed aloud as he thought of the date: In thirty-five days on the Fourth of July, he and Lenore would get married. It was no secret that four love affairs obsessed him: Lenore, his friends and family, his God—and the U.S. Navy F/A-18 Hornet fighter jet.

Mike stretched his nearly six-foot height to push against the end of the antique frame he had refinished for their marriage bed. Vital and strong, he opened himself to whatever the day might hold.

In the stillness of the California pre-dawn, the new day quivered in his waking consciousness like the charged atmosphere of a great orchestra in that moment just before the first note. Each eye, each ear, each muscle waits for the signal. There is no turning back. No restless movement. No question as to what will follow. The conductor lifts the baton. The musicians wait . . .

That moment was no different for Mike. He loved life; he believed in its fulfilling God's plan. It was as though his eyes, his ears, his muscles waited for the next signal. There was no turning back. No restless movement. The only question was *what* in God's plan would follow. God lifted the baton. Mike waited . . .

Jumping out of bed, he grinned aloud—Mike could do that. The faintest smile spread inside out until the guffaw crinkled around his eyes before the sound burst its seams. He was counting the days now. Soon, he'd begin each day in Lenore's arms.

Moments later he heard the phone ringing. Dripping wet, his heart thumping with anticipation, he raced from the shower to answer. It would be Lenore. In a few weeks she would finish teaching in Nashville before their summer wedding. Then the hundreds of dollars in monthly phone bills between Nashville and Lemoore would melt to nothing. At last they could reach out and touch each other without paying for it.

Lifting the receiver, he cleared his husky morning voice that would tell her again how much he loved her. That big, silly grin widened between his ears as he pictured her dark sleepy eyes and gentle curves. But all he heard was a click. Maybe it was a wrong number. He decided not to risk waking her if she were asleep.

While packing his lunch he listened to the weather forecast—a perfect day. In three hours he'd be airborne over the majestic Sierra. Mike thought flying jets was one of God's better gifts to the human race and didn't hesitate letting anyone know how he felt about it. For years he'd lived for the day he would climb into the cockpit of an F-18 fighter-jet.

Witnessing God's help in arriving at this milestone, after that first flight he wrote, "Awesome! I'm humbled that God would allow me to do this! Training is fast and furious, but I love it!"

Always pushing to reach the next goal in each phase of training, he often reminded himself, "*Today* is great. I can live *this* day to the max and not wish for tomorrow, because when it gets here, today will be gone forever." Barely two months earlier, the pressures of seven years' preparation dissolved in the excitement of receiving his coveted gold wings pinned on fliers who earn them.

Finally assigned to Squadron VFA-125 at Lemoore Naval Air Station (NAS), he began training as a replacement pilot (RP). RPs succeed pilots who have completed the demands of rigorous training. Hours of study, practice on the simulator and completion of assigned missions consumed him. Working and studying 14-16 hours a day, he wrote he had only scratched the surface. "It's kinda difficult to drink from a fire hose," he said, "but I sure am learning!"

Clearly, the F-18 had hooked Mike. Soon he'd complete this phase, too, and take Lenore to Lemoore. He often laughed about that. The names of his lover and the naval air station even rhymed. He found himself comparing his loves. "Airplanes don't compare with women," he said, "but what a great combination." His love affairs obsessed him. They flowed together through his life as one mighty river, inseparable, powerful.

At 6:00 A.M. Mike locked the door to the apartment and headed for his motorcycle. Securing his helmet and gripping the handle bars, his sturdy biceps rippled beneath a California tan. Along with years of physical and mental conditioning, Mike had long ago initiated the routines and life-style that sculpted his body. He heard the cycle respond to his touch as did the F-18, the Fuego and, in fact, as did every piece of machinery that he mastered. Leaning into the breeze, he drove into the cool dawn of another of God's days.

A Marine who was one day closer to his goal of fighter jet pilot, Mike had logged in nearly 300 total flight hours, with only 20.5 in the F-18. It wasn't much in contrast to his instructor pilot (IP) who had more than 1,150 hours in the fighter/attack plane, but he was getting there. The IP racked up hours one at a time, just as he did.

At 7:00 A.M. Mike met with his IP, Captain Ginsberg. Mike had been scheduled to fly the event a day earlier, but it was cancelled and rescheduled for May 20. The brief was uneventful. Weather was estimated at a 3,000 foot ceiling, 20,000 feet overcast, visibility 7 miles, all within regulations. He would use visual flight rules (VFR) rather than instrument flight rules (IFR).

By 7:30 A.M. Mike was suiting up in the garb marked *Mueller*. He wiggled into the snug torso harness. It connects to the Martin-Baker seat and parachute and also acts as a shoulder belt when landing, especially needed when the pilot slams onto 600 feet of deck space on a rocking carrier ship at sea.

Over the flight suit Mike pulled on the g-suit. It automatically inflates air bladders around the thighs, calves and abdominal areas to squeeze the blood upward into vital organs. Without it, dangerous side effects of flying at high speeds and elevations create loss of blood flow to the brain, causing pilots to become disoriented or to pass out. While "pulling 4 g's," the chin feels glued to the chest, arms feel nailed to the lap, and it's no wonder: A 100-pound person weighs the equivalent of 400 pounds.

Mike's descriptions of his flight gear could spin a web

that caught listeners and held them captive. But, like other pilots, after a few flights he seldom thought about the details or the personal survival kit, from its oxygen tank to signaling devices, from a medical packet to Charms candy. Mike joked about hoping he'd never need to eat those Charms—pilots don't really expect to use the survival kit.

On the way out to his morning flight, Mike joked with Criello. They'd gone through The Basic School for Marines at Quantico, Virginia, and all flight training together. Criello had watched Mike for years. His buddies couldn't get him to drink anything stronger than a chocolate milkshake or Coke. He knew Mike as someone who was ecstatic even about routine flights.

Mike had summarized both his love for the plane and for the majestic mountains when he wrote, "We fly over the Sierras, which I love! The F-18 is incredible! I can't believe how blessed I am . . ."

At 7:50 A.M. Ginsberg and Mueller walked to their assigned F-18, Raider 58, for a pre-flight check. *Front seat for me!* Fully aware of climbing into that prized position, Mike would soon fly a single-seater without an IP sitting behind him to observe, prompt and grade him. He had prepared well to be tested on the advanced Hughes radar system and successfully completed the oral quizzing on the introduction to air-to-ground radar. He was ready to test it out. But he also knew that no matter how many times the aviator flies, each flight is a test, a performance, an opportunity to prove the pilot has *the right stuff.*

Mike knew, God being his helper, that he was among that elite number.

That had been three hours earlier.

* * * * *

Then, the announcement came. It reverberated around Lemoore Naval Air Station. Crashing headlong into the aviators' churning apprehension, it was no longer a possibility, but a real event: *Missing aircraft*.

The interminable day lengthened into darkness. To the North, the night thickened with snow blowing across the cadaverous Eastern Sierra that Mike loved.

CHAPTER 2

RAIDER 58: MISSING

As for God
his way is perfect . . .
—Psalm 18:30

It was spring in Bartlesville, Oklahoma. On the evening of May 20, 1987, two Marine officers drove north from Broken Arrow Marine Base to deliver a message. They had rehearsed it often. They had performed it in other times and in other places. They would do it again. But it did not come easily.

Pulling into the shade across the road from 1800 Polaris Drive, they glanced toward the inviting gray limestone house settled among green shrubs and vines. Inside, Mike's parents Don and Naomi had just finished supper. A knock interrupted the evening news. Swinging open the heavy wood door, Naomi saw two uniformed Marines.

"Good evening. Mrs. Mueller? Is your husband also home?" one asked.

"Why . . . yes." Their approach caught her off guard. They were accustomed to friends, and even strangers, dropping in for friendly conversation, food, and fun, just because they knew Mike or his sisters. Her eyes glimpsed the official Marine Corps truck parked across the road. Its massive dark form silhouetted against chartreuse foliage momentarily mesmerized her.

Why did they ask if Don is home? "Please, come in." She preceded them past the living room with its grand piano and the kitchen where a nineteen-inch mounted bass hangs behind the breakfast bar. Mike's first catch, it is dated October 23, 1966.

Don stood up to meet them and switched off the news. "Won't you sit down?" he began in his quiet, friendly manner. Don began to speculate: *These guys must know Mike. Wonder why they're so formal.*

Ignoring Don's invitation to sit down, one began abruptly, "Your son's plane, Sir, is missing from a routine training flight over the Sierras."

A mental short-circuit left the parents simply standing there. The young officers never knew what, exactly, to expect when they gave the news.

"They left the Naval Air Station at Lemoore at 0838 hours and were expected to return at 1020," the other Marine explained.

"Three other F-18 pilots returned on time."

Cold fingers of terror tightened around the tiny human cluster, still standing, still talking, almost nonchalantly. As if watching a play from a distant balcony, Naomi saw herself in the drama. She heard her absurdly calm voice ask, "When did they begin to search?"

"They try to give the pilots a wide time allowance before they begin. The first search and rescue aircraft left at 1300 hours, Ma'am."

"They've reported snows, Ma'am, even this late in May in the Sierras."

Naomi had thrown a lifeline to her composure. "Of course," she smiled at the young officers, "God is with them. I bet they've ejected. We'll get a call soon and . . ." Naomi didn't finish, but her effervescence, positive thinking, and faith clicked into automatic.

Don quietly inquired whether anyone else was in the plane.

"The instructor pilot, Sir, is Captain Daniel Ginsberg."

Suddenly, they were gone. Naomi turned to Don. Alone again, they clung to each other. *As for God, his way is perfect.* Naomi often quotes the scripture verse that first comforted her. No reason to panic. God is in control. They decided Don would stay near the phone and Naomi would go to church as planned. They agreed not to mention the news to anyone until they had more information.

"But, shall we call the girls?" Naomi asked, referring to Mike's two sisters and Lenore.

"Let's wait till we hear something," Don suggested, meaning, of course, *Let's wait till we hear something good.* Sketchy details allowed them to hope.

"We'll just go on as usual. I'll bring home our house guest from the visiting choir. Then, I'll cut out my dress for the wedding," Naomi announced. With Mike and Lenore's wedding only six weeks away, many details needed attention.

* * * * *

Arriving at her Nashville apartment about 10:30 that night, Lenore listened to the telephoned message. "I have something important to tell you," Naomi had said in a controlled voice. "Call anytime you get in." Expecting to talk about wedding plans, Lenore dialed and heard Naomi begin.

"Lenore, Mike's plane didn't get back from a routine flight this morning."

"What do you mean? I just talked to him last night." Lenore felt a whirring inside her brain, like the works of a giant clock going awry. Without connection. Without meaning. Such news throws out non sequiturs, like: *I just talked to him last night*. Or, *We ate breakfast together this morning*. Or, *I just received a letter from her today*.

"We don't know what to do except pray," Naomi continued. "Probably good news will come before morning."

Naomi's positive calm poured across the wires, oozing into the cracks in Lenore's control. "We'll call you right away when we hear something," she promised. "It's all in God's hands. His way is perfect!"

Lenore and Mike had talked the previous night, sharing their dreams for their marriage and depth of feeling for each other. An uncomfortable, unidentified feeling had prompted her to call before he left for the base that very day, but there was no answer. She had just wanted to tell him again how much she loved him. Although certain Mike had ejected, she still fought off the torment of these odds: Of those who eject, one in ten is killed.

After calling her parents to pray, Lenore waited alone through that interminable night. Memories and prayers swirled around her. She felt nothing, she felt everything. With her feet curled up beneath her on her rocking chair, she sat all night with her arms wrapped around her teddy bear, sobbing. She sobbed until the tear ducts dried up and her eyelashes disappeared.

* * * * *

In California that afternoon of May 20, Marilyn Ginsberg hurried to answer her doorbell. Like a series of freeze-frame images that she will replay for the rest of her life, Marilyn sometimes still watches herself in those moments.

Through the window in the front door, she saw two uniformed figures. Weakness flooded every cell. Staggering closer to open the door, she saw their faces, and she knew. Even before they said it, she knew what they had rehearsed to tell her. A sharp scream thrust itself out of the scabbard of her soul to pierce the closed door. Images and sounds penetrated her memory in a fuzzy, unfocused frenzy, unreal, incomprehensible. A boy toddler tugged at her leg. A baby girl cried.

Then mercifully, shock and hope wrapped around her

like a cloak to save her sanity. She clung to her husband's record: *He's an A-1, Top Gun instructor pilot. Surely the two men are alive. They would be rescued soon.*

* * * * *

Living in Springfield, Virginia, I still knew nothing extraordinary had happened on May 20. It came and went without my recognizing its impact on the rest of my life. But I recall that Thursday night of May 21 as though it were happening now.

The call came from my sister-in-law Marj from Texas. Marj's family had lived in Bartlesville and knew Mike's family well. Her son Alan and Mike were close friends.

"Did you hear the news yet?" she asked. My brain scanned the national news I'd heard at 10. Nothing registered. "Uh, what news?"

"Mike's plane disappeared yesterday."

Speechless, I listened as she continued. My heart thumped madly, out of control. I traced blue veins in my hands. I sucked in quick, shallow gasps and pictured Mike floating under an open parachute.

"Well, he loved parachuting—" I bit my lip when a nervous laugh escaped. Sharon walked through the kitchen. Sixteen, blonde, pretty, sleepy. I flashed a big smile at my youngest child to cover my fear and confusion. I was glad to be talking on the phone. How would I tell her? Her 25-year-old, brother-like Marine pilot buddy. A picture of Mike and Sharon on his motorcycle was posted on the refrigerator. But now he could be lying in a frozen mass of wreckage . . .

NO! My mind screamed against such thoughts. "With all their training, and the technology of those planes, you know he has to be all right," I later told my husband Ray, expecting him to reassure me. But he said nothing and held me close. When we climbed the stairs for the night, I was relieved to see Sharon already asleep. I hoped our other daughter Marcia was asleep, too. Just home from college, Marcia had that day received a letter from Mike, forwarded from her college address.

"I'm so thankful God has given me the opportunity to fly F-18's," Mike had written.

Throughout the long night, the news about Mike's disappearance draped heavily across me. I felt like a tiny ant bearing a weighty load. Finally, a whippoorwill serenaded the dawn. *So, it was real, was it? Not a nightmare?* No phone call with good news had rescued me. He must still be missing. Or worse. It would soon be 48 hours since he disappeared. The darkness licked my face as a thousand dead-end questions rolled endlessly in the corridor of my consciousness.

I sneaked slowly from bed and felt for the bathroom light. "Are you okay, Marf?" Ray's voice startled me. He said he did not fall asleep until after four o'clock. He was thinking about Mike.

"Remember how I always teased Mike about sleeping in on Saturdays while I was out jogging at 5 in the morning?" he asked me.

"In your dreams," I answered, bending to kiss him. Mike had belonged. He understood our family, our humor. He was part of us.

A neighbor's car charged the pre-dawn quiet. I recalled another early morning sound when Mike revved up the engine of his little white Renault. The girls and I had taken off with him, just for fun, with the wind blowing through the sun roof. We played all day at King's Dominion, screaming deliciously on the wildest roller coaster and drying in the scorching sun after getting soaked on the log flume. Mike asked me to drive home—the tough Marine was so tired from playing. We laughed a lot that day.

My grin startled me in the mirror's reflection. *Why am I laughing? How is it that tears and laughter court each other?* I pressed my fingers into my temples, still hurting from tears shed and unshed. *How long do they search for a missing pilot? Of course, they never give up. He'll be found today! He ejected on time.*

In the kitchen I pulled some yeast dough from the refrigerator where it had risen slowly through the night. My hands embraced it. Kneading . . . . pushing . . . shaping . . . The ordinary seemed alive, inviting. Nothing seemed real, yet everything seemed vividly real.

Michael-memories washed over me like giant waves. I struggled to gulp air before the next big one came.

Suddenly, I was afraid I'd forget how he looked. I'd never thought about that while he was in Florida, or Texas, or California. I clung desperately to his image. Then panic lunged at me.

O God, help me! What if it were Ray? How could I go on living if it were Ray? How could I give up my spouse? my parents? the children who grew inside me? How do I give up anyone so loved?

Recalling a story from out of *The Hiding Place* comforted me. When Corrie ten Boom was a child, she visited a bereaved family with her father and was terrified to see the still, blue body of the dead child laid out nearby. Crying for answers to my kinds of questions, she waited while her gentle father searched for them. Then he asked, "When we ride the train, Corrie, when do I hand you your ticket?"

"When we get on the train, Papa," she answered.

Tears washed my puffy eyes again. *Of course. When the time comes, I can do it.* Comfort snuggled me as I kneaded and thought, prayed and waited. Messy, floured counter top. Warm, heavy dough. Quiet, safe kitchen. I thought about my frequent conversations with Mike about safety. Whenever he told me of new and dangerous assignments, I'd ask, "Oh Mike, is it safe?" Laughing, he always responded, "Safe? Of course! How could I not be safe in God's hands?" Did Mike see the bigger picture? Young as he was, he seemed to understand—but did I?

I remembered Mike's last phone call to me. Less than two weeks earlier, the phone woke us about 1 A.M. He laughed about flying, wedding details, plans to visit his buddy Lance in Hawaii and about meeting us when we flew to California in August.

Then he paused. "I wanted to say thank you before Mother's Day is over," he said, suddenly serious.

"But it *is* over. Remember, it's Monday morning here!" I teased him.

If only he would call again . . . I blotted tears on my robe sleeve and punched the dough harder. I punched the pain and smashed the doubt and crushed the agony into the yeasty dough. I then watched my hands shape the dough into smooth loaves. Suddenly a presence interrupted my reverie. I was not alone. I felt Mike behind me. I turned to look, unafraid, expectant. I reached out to touch him. Mike was present. Beyond sight, beyond physical touch, yet he was more present to me than his body to embrace.

Mike is with me, and I am not afraid, I thought. Awareness of his presence faded, but that moment sustained me. Had his spirit been set free to come to me because he had died? Or, was his presence a kind of communication as he waited for rescue? I couldn't grasp what it meant, but the fact of Mike's presence in those moments confirmed my faith: We are spirit; we are eternal; God cares. Even in the midst of tragedy, life goes on. Bread still rises. These things I knew.

Thank God, Mike, you're alive. Alive!

But what did that mean? I intended to find out.

CHAPTER 3

BEGINNING THE SEARCH

You have kept count of my tossings;
put my tears in your bottle . . .
in God I trust; I am not afraid.
—Psalm 56:8, 11 (NRSV)

By 1:30 in the afternoon of the first day, the assigned Search and Rescue (SAR) coordinator at the Scott Air Force Base Aerospace Rescue and Recovery Center (ARRC) initiated the first sortie. The pilots searched for six hours, at great personal risk, until efforts were suspended due to hazardous terrain, imminent nightfall and deteriorating weather: snow, low cloud ceilings, icing.

By the end of the second day, family members and friends began arriving in California to join Marilyn Ginsberg and the military in the search. Just before leaving for California, Don sat down to read Mike's letter, written Saturday:

> I had my check ride yesterday, so I am now a full-fledged Hornet driver! Things are still moving right along, but I'm keeping up . . . Thank you so much for your love and support! You'll never know how much I appreciate and love you! I think you're the perfect

parents, and I'm looking forward to a great time in July! . . .

Don didn't dare think six weeks ahead. Within hours, he and Naomi were flying 31,000 feet above the Sierra Nevada range that Mike loved and had flown over a day earlier. Arriving at Mike's apartment and seeing his familiar white Renault, Don gasped. He couldn't help wondering, *Is it all a mistake? Has he returned?*

Mike's two sisters and fiance arrived together. They had met unexpectedly enroute to the Denver airport, having miraculously scheduled the same flight. They talked and prayed, cried and crocheted all the way to Fresno.

In Mike's apartment the freezer and refrigerator were well-stocked, as though he'd expected them. Remembering the past and believing in the future, they broke bread together. The rolls, sausage cheese biscuits and banana bread Mike had made became a ritual of connection with the missing Marine.

Always at home among the academic books on his table, Mike's Bible lay open to Psalm 139:

> Where can I go from your Spirit? Where can I flee from your presence? If I go up to the heavens, you are there. If I make my bed in the depths, you are there. If I rise on the wings of the dawn, if I settle on the far side of the sea, even there your hand will guide me; your right hand will hold me fast . . .

No doubt about it. Mike lived by faith in this sovereign God.

*****

The Ginsberg home became the hub of activity for family and friends. Unlike spouses of military mishap aviators whose planes are located, Marilyn was soon feverishly following every lead that pointed to solving the mystery. She did not accept the notion they had crashed, or at least had not ejected.

The pilots who searched understood that their own lives might depend on uncovering the truth about what had happened to the missing men—and why.

Finding Dan Ginsberg and Mike Mueller demanded their intense concentration. From sunup to sundown, SAR sorties exceeded the usual numbers. Dozens of helicopters and fixed wing aircraft participated, flying from NAS Fallon and Lemoore, from Nevada and California Civil Air Patrol (CAP) and from Fort Irwin, Moffett Field, and the Reno Army National Guard.

Interspersed among the public military reports were rumors about the pilots having been ordered to special missions, not only kept secret from the families, but also surreptitiously planned without informing the participants until the last minute. Others considered the possibility of enemy interference for the purpose of obtaining top-secret information and equipment. Even more bizarre was this theory: The pilots had been captured by a drug ring.

While everyone was discussing and reasoning, so visibly consumed with the task at hand, on the inside each continued a private search sustained by conversations with the missing men—or their God.

> *Where on earth are you, Dan? How could you do this to me? Please come back to me, Michael. You know I can't live without you . . . With your record, you couldn't have made a huge mistake . . . Hey, man, a Top-Gun guy like you had to see it coming and eject . . . Hang in there, guys. We'll find you! O God, please, please guide them to search the right places today . . .*

Interior conversations like these continually intersected the military jargon, the tears, the laughter. It's the kind of thing everybody does, but nobody talks about.

Instead, they calmly discussed tangible, surface matters: records of the two aviators; reports of lightning; explosion sounds; the last known position (LKP) marked on tracking maps of the Eastern Sierra; hundreds of lakes, any of which could be hiding the plane; a reported 12-15 hundred gallon fuel reserve; radio contact with Raider 58 by the other pilots; engine operating time and safety records for the F-18 in general and Raider 58 in particular; mechanical problems and flame out; survival training; emergency procedures and volunteers for the daily searches. Continually reasoning and figuring, they believed that some clue, somebody, would crack the mystery at any moment.

Investigators combed the records to find any indication that either pilot exhibited careless or hazardous patterns in their personal or professional lives that would indicate emotional instability or unsuitable personal habits. Like one more hook on which the families and friends could continue to hang their hopes, Dan Ginsberg's record spoke for itself. A Top Gun pilot, he had flown the 1986 bombing raid over Libya. One of the most experienced F-18 Hornet pilots in the squadron, he'd been the first in his class of Navy pilots to fly the F-18. "Flawless, superlative, prudent conservative judgment" characterized his performance.

Typical of his caution, Ginsberg had recently refused to return to base due to his assessment of an "inadequate fuel reserve," although in many instances other pilots had returned with less; twelve days earlier he had refused to fly two pilots who needed to return from NAS Fallon because the weather was marginal. Mike's record reflected equal prudence and competence. Squadron members stressed he was studious, conscientious, emotionally well-balanced and of impeccable character and lifestyle. Lenore and Marilyn, interrogated on their relationships with the missing men and their conversations the night before they disappeared, assured the investigators that neither had any personal problems.

Against the backdrop of these unusual circumstances, two toddlers wandered and played, ate and napped. Ben at two years and Jessica Ginsberg at eleven months, didn't know their daddy was missing. They didn't understand that after days of searches and expert military investigation, an awareness that Ginsberg and Mueller might not return was threatening to smother all hope like a giant gray pall. That growing perception mushroomed into a mandate to continue the search for as long as it would take.

Of course, acute shock still protected the families trying to grasp even the idea that their loved ones were *missing*. Such a euphemism was easy enough to anchor them when no crash site, no bodies, and no sign of the missing pilots had surfaced. They mentally rehearsed the moment the news would come. Depending on the fluctuating mood of a given moment, sometimes the imaginary response was controlled and accepting; sometimes aloof and disbelieving; sometimes hysterical and raging. But it didn't matter at all, because the call never came.

* * * * *

At Lemoore Naval Air Station, the names *Mueller* and *Ginsberg* posted over two hooks waited as empty, foreboding reminders that the personal flight gear the men had removed on Wednesday morning had been missing for too long. Their comrades only glanced sideways at Mike and Dan's pictures on the wall with other Squadron 125 members, as though staring at them might somehow cast a spell. On their way to becoming Navy fighter pilots, two brand-new, young RP's passed the photos and empty hooks without a glance on their way to becoming Navy fighter pilots.

By May 25 all leads had been followed and all grids searched and re-searched by high numbers of aircraft—37 on that day alone—in addition to CAP ground forces. Two words had been whispered within the squadron, words most of the searchers could not accept: *pilot error*. How could pilot error for these particular men on a routine training flight possibly figure into the scenario?

Of course, Ginsberg rode the back seat. But not only does

the instructor pilot continually assess, inform, and advise the student pilot, any procedure can be rectified by the instructor pilot as necessary.

Finally, Commander Johnson broke the worst possible conclusion to the families. The pilots had likely made an error in deciding to continue to fly in very bad weather, had probably been flying at low altitudes and crashed into a mountain peak that was snow-covered and obscured by clouds. Having received no distress signal that would have been initiated upon impact, and finding no sign of aircraft wreckage, the Navy saw no possibility of their survival. There. He had said it.

Yet, what the media and the military assumed from this clinical report was more than the families and friends could accept. By the end of the first week, newspapers across the country announced the search for the missing Navy jet was suspended. The military was ready to move on. The pilots were missing and presumed dead. Avoiding it was no longer an option. Lenore and the others began to plan the unthinkable: a memorial service for their missing loved ones at the Naval Air Station at Lemoore.

Across the country, people still prayed. In Oklahoma, many insisted Mike was alive. Back East, Department of Defense (DOD) officials examined the data. In California, Memorial Day weekend plowed into the families with a vengeance.

* * * * *

Family members and friends gathered on May 26 for a reception at the base before the military memorial service. A warm breeze and blue skies, friendly chatter and laughter set the stage, as for a wedding.

But something pointed to the difference. Parked across the wide expanse of tarmac, the F-18 Hornets that Mike loved reminded the hundreds gathered there of the reason they had come. Confusing and inconclusive as they were, each passing moment, each day that ended, pointed to what none wanted to believe, yet gathered to commemorate.

Lenore's huge dark eyes searched the crowd, looking for someone who understood how *she* felt. Ragged emotions stalked her composure. Laughter and hugs passed freely back and forth through a thin membrane called denial for some, and acceptance for others. Marilyn as the assumed widow, her children, the four parents, brothers and sisters of the missing pilots, and even friends, belonged to the scene in a way that Lenore did not.

Wrapped in imagination, Lenore could look down at the crowd as though from a great distance. *Don't they know Mike is still alive?* Standing there with Mike, together they watched their families and friends milling about. He held her close. He understood. She knew she was more than family, more than a friend. She meant more to him than anyone in the world. In less than six weeks they would become as one.

Clinging to such thoughts as a rock climber clings to handholds, she hoisted herself above the crowd and commotion on memories of caresses and kisses, of laughter and letters.

"In the last two years," she later said, "I knew him better than anyone. Scores of times he said to me, 'Lenore, I would give up flying; I'd even give up the Marine Corps for you. You are second only to God who is the most important one in the world to me.'"

Don walked toward her, breaking her lonely reverie. "Will you have some punch, Lenore?" The question seemed to take her by surprise. Her food and drink did not consist of what they served. During her musing it seemed the clock had stopped. Nothing had changed around her. People still milled about. Many smiled, hugged her, said they were praying. She smoothed her tea rose pink top and rubbed her cold hands across her flowing white skirt. She pressed her purse close to her breast. It held their engagement photo and Mike's last letter.

The time had come. Mike's father stood quietly beside her and offered his arm. Naomi preceded them on the arm of a Marine escort. The chapel was packed. The Admiral of the Pacific Fleet and other officers joined them to listen to comforting scriptures and familiar Marine and Navy hymns.

During the vitae read for each pilot, I recalled a story about Mike, a child who was born to fly. One day when guests were present at dinner, he announced, "Dad, I want to buy a plane." Mike was 16 then. His enthusiasm for flying was boundless. "I already checked it out—and it only costs $10,000!" Relief that they could head him off a little longer showed in Naomi's laughing response, "Oh, that's *much* too cheap! We can't have you flying a plane that only costs $10,000! That's not nearly good enough for you." The guests laughed. Mike waited. He had recently written, "The systems on the jet are amazing. I'm beginning to see why one of these costs $25 million." He'd come a long way.

Chaplain Ryder called attention back to the present: Both aviators had left lovers and families without a final word; without a last embrace or final farewell. He said the two comrades epitomized both youth and the red on our flag. Mike's former pastor, John Snook, read from Ecclesiastes 7:13-14 and encouraged the mourners to "consider God" as comforter, restorer and Savior. The four folded flags on the altar were later presented to the parents of the men, to Marilyn and to Lenore.

Several hundred people gathered outside for the final symbolic moment. Four F-18 Hornets bombarded their senses. The ground shook. The thundering majesty absorbed the sound of each pounding heart. One plane, then another, broke from formation to veer sharply from sight, sound, and presence with them. A new awareness that two of their own had indeed disappeared swallowed them up. Unbidden tears washed over the missing pilots' mothers, sisters, fathers, lovers, friends—and crisply uniformed Marines.

* * * * *

After the service, hundreds of friends gathered in Marilyn's house and back yard. Although they had not sung together for many years, Lenore and her a capella group sang for Marilyn, *Amazing Grace*. For the first time during her dark night, Lenore felt God's presence.

Her sister Katrina Stonoff is a journalist from Arizona. She wrote for *the sun* newspaper about "the very military, red, white and blue, July Fourth wedding" planned for her baby sister and Mike. She revealed feelings that simmered beneath what was obvious to onlookers that Memorial Day weekend. "Rumors run rampant; emotions sky-rocket, then plummet as expert and novice alike speculate," she wrote. Katrina with her parents and sisters had traveled to Lemoore to wait while their husbands stayed home to care for babies, businesses and animals. The siblings had not been together with their parents for years. Bonds were strengthened with the Marine officers, friends, and one another. "Suddenly," Katrina wrote, "it seems we understand each other . . . And we say words we often fail to say: *I love you*."

Paradoxically, like other families in desperate situations, laughter interrupted their tears. "We joke and tease and flirt with the Marines. Seconds later, we weep and ask the unanswerable *why*," Katrina wrote. "None of us wants to return home [where] we get distracted and forget to mourn or hope or pray."

Each was deathly afraid to forget. Teetering on the brink of realistic thinking, they told themselves the chances the men survived were slim, yet they feared if they forgot, even for a moment, Mike would surely die, and it would be their fault. "So we try to remember all the time," Katrina wrote. "We cry into the dishwater. We pray at the photographic enlarger. We hope while driving to the grocery store . . . A life force that strong, with that much to live for, cannot be dead."

Friends from across the country called daily with

excitement. "This is the day," they announced to the families. "We can feel it. Mike is coming back today." Katrina, too, found herself singing from the musical *Annie*, and believing it: *The sun'll come out tomorrow.*

"I can feel it," she said. "Tomorrow's the day. Mike's coming home tomorrow."

CHAPTER 4

WAITING FOR A WEDDING

. . . an instant end to all their happiness,
an eternity of terror.
Their present life is only a dream!
They will waken to the truth as one awakens
from a dream of things that never really were.
—Psalm 73:19-20 (TLB)

Like a lost and lonely child, Lenore waited. Without a home, a job, a purpose, she felt as though she were dangling from a fragile thread of her unraveling tapestry of a future with Mike. Her wedding gown waited in a closet; a ring still circled her finger; her arms ached to hold more than a pillow through each long night.

Arriving at Mike's apartment before the memorial service, Lenore stayed with the Muellers in the intended honeymoon house. She touched what Mike had just touched and ate what he had prepared. She slept in the bed Mike had refinished, and on the same sheets where Mike had written her just days earlier: "I've been lying here in bed wishing you were here with me." She lost more than fifteen pounds in the first week.

Lenore opened Mike's accumulating mail: Aunt Cara Lee wrote she would play the organ for the wedding; friends Alan and Linda planned on a December ski trip with them; Ginny Krenning addressed her envelope: Mike Mueller, Awesome Aviator; Dick Steinberg addressed his letter: General Mike Mueller.

Finding Mike's pink shirt that he had worn and thrown into the hamper, Lenore began sleeping with it. He had worn it for their engagement picture. She inhaled the Old Spice scent and felt his closeness until one morning she could no longer smell it. Frantic, she felt him slipping away. Clutching frantically at memories, she cried out, "I can't remember how he felt when I held him, or what his voice sounds like. I feel like I'm falling off a cliff. I can't hang on anymore."

During those six weeks leading up to the wedding weekend, she often drove Mike's car into the country with the sun roof open and the radio blaring. Questions shattering her customary control, she cried out, "O God! How could you do this to me?" Then she screamed at Mike, "How could *you* do this to me? You knew we were getting married. Why weren't you more careful?" Hysterically, she pulled to the side of the road, unable to see, her body shaking with sobs.

At other times she groped quietly for answers to her frustrations. Her extreme mood swings frightened her. She heard herself begging God to take her life; she wondered how to do it herself, questioning why she should live.

"Waiting is more difficult than getting the news someone you love has died," Lenore said. "That conflict of hope and hopelessness fight each other constantly." She lay across her bed for hours with her hand cradling the phone, trying to fall asleep, yet afraid to do so.

"I was always waiting . . . waiting for him to call, saying he was locked out of the apartment; or for the military to call with the news that they had found the men," she said. Forced to deal with their possible deaths, one night she wrote this psalm of agony:

My God, my God! Why hast thou forsaken me?
I cry to you from the lowest of lows.

My soul is so weak, my heart is broken.
All strength is gone from my body. Help me!
In all my life I have never felt
such despair, such agony, such aloneness.
I wish you would take me to my eternal home.
How long must my soul anguish?
How long must my soul wait?
Hear my cry, O Lord. Give rest to my weary bones.
There is nothing but you left. Only you and me.
All my hopes and dreams have been torn away.
Help me. Hear my cry.

As though feeling her way through a dense fog, she hugged the path, straining to see any familiar landmark, struggling to get somewhere while its damp chill of solitude and darkness swirled around her. Yet in the midst of the fog, she was also dimly aware of so many people, so much to do, so many plans to make, files to find, dishes to wash for all the guests, meetings to attend with military personnel, discussions with searchers, time with Marilyn, her family, the Muellers, friends—and even the wedding party who had arrived to walk with her through the haze.

Following the military memorial service in California, her mother remained with her in the honeymoon apartment an extra week; her sister visited for about a month. Her friends Kelly and Verlyn packed her belongings in Nashville and stored them at their house. Her car waited in the garage at the school where she taught. Life was on hold as she waited for results of the massive military searches.

*****

Before Mike disappeared, strange dreams and premonitions had fallen like shadows across letters and conversations. Mike had told Lenore he would give anything if they could skip the next few months. Lenore's father had a premonition three times about Mike's disappearance. An Academy classmate was so startled he woke up his wife after he dreamed Mike's plane crashed.

Prophetic irony shaded Lenore's letter to Naomi in March, just after Mike's winging. Of course, neither one caught its significance then. She wrote, "I'm learning to depend on God. I'm thankful that both of you, and my own parents, support me in love and prayer . . . " Oddly, she quoted from Luke 1:78-79: " . . . the sunrise from on high shall visit us, to shine upon those who sit in darkness and the shadow of death . . ."

Even the ordered wedding cake—in the shape of an F-18—symbolized what was to be. Mottled sky-blue and cloud-white, their wedding invitations also reflected Mike's favorite place. Their love for each other, for God and for flying shaped a trinity that permeated their relationship.

One day while in the kitchen alone, God's presence startled Lenore. The room brightened brilliantly. Awed, she beckoned her niece Summer to come quickly. A favorite of Mike's, she was six years old then. "What is it?" Summer cried. Lenore gasped, "Jesus is here!" They knelt together to thank him. Even now, Summer sometimes reminds her, "Remember when Jesus came to see us?"

Reading Mike's love letters by the hundreds also helped anchor Lenore to sanity through the summer. They had talked by phone every night and written to each other every day. Lenore both giggled and cried her way through them. His mind had definitely shifted ahead to their married life.

> I love you . . . I'm dying to hold you. I must warn you, I'm going to want to be very romantic when you visit. We'll spend at least one night in the yard. I've spent many beautiful moonlit nights off the [Corpus Christi] bay by myself, dreaming of sharing it.

Five weeks before May 20, he wrote:

> I'm thankful I won't have this void in my life much longer. God sure knew what he was doing when he drew

up the plans for you . . . I thank God for putting these drives in us while we save ourselves for each other. How I love you and thirst for you. I want to fill myself with you and I want you to give yourself to me. What an awesome wife God is blessing me with . . .

One afternoon while washing the car, Mike heard Stevie Wonder sing about his part-time lover and found himself repeatedly humming the catchy tune and singing the words. Its message suddenly angered him and he wrote Lenore:

Music is powerful . . . If I'm going to fill my mind with something, not only do I not want it to be raunchy and immoral, but I don't even want it to be mediocre! I want it to help me be peaceful inside, to encourage me, and to radiate from me so I can encourage others! . . . I want what I hear at home and on my own time to be edifying.

. . . I don't just want to be faithful to you physically, but also mentally! That's not an easy task these days! But that's what I am going to do! If I fill my mind with scripture and encouraging words, there will be a lot less room for garbage . . . 42 days, Doll!!! I am so ecstatic and can hardly wait. I love you so much and it is such a pleasure to love you and be loved by you!! Thanks for letting me share with you and be honest with you. I want to do all I can to make our marriage strong, wonderful and beautiful!

Then on May 5, two weeks before he disappeared in Raider 58, he wrote, calling her his dearest and most incredible and awesome wife. "I am so busy now, but by the time you get here, things will be slowing down. Except then . . . " Lenore giggled. Then, her giggles turned to tears as she read on:

When I flew in the Sierra mountains today, I saw all kinds of isolated lakes and just dreamed of camping there in the beautiful country with beautiful you. I'm crazy about you, Love. I wish I could come to you Memorial Day weekend . . . Lenore, you are the love of my life, forever. God bless you, Doll. Totally committed, I'm mad about you.

Of course, May 20 arrived before that Memorial Day weekend in 1987. Lenore never dreamed that anything could interfere with their idealized love. The gruelling stretch to the wedding weekend finally culminated for her in the trip back to Bartlesville—without Mike. How do you prepare for a wedding when the groom is missing?

* * * * *

Their love had developed slowly from puppy love to prenuptial passion. Years earlier on the way home from a youth convention, Lenore and five other high school students stopped at Bartlesville Wesleyan College because a blizzard was on the way. Following church the next day, the Muellers invited the group to have lunch with them. Mike rounded up friends to take the guests sledding and roller skating. Lenore told her friend Donna after that weekend, "I'm going to marry that Mike Mueller some day."

During many off-again, on-again years, neither was ready for commitment to a serious relationship. Finally, at Mike's winging they set the wedding date for the Fourth of July, 1987.

With Lenore teaching in Nashville and Mike in jet training in Beeville, Texas, they spent little time together. But they dreamed big. Lenore would be a homemaker, learn to fly, have babies—in that order. Together they would teach Officers Christian Fellowship Bible study and host it in their home.

* * * * *

Meanwhile, the wedding day arrived. With so many ties in Bartlesville for both Mike and Lenore, they had planned to celebrate their vows in Mike's home church. The wedding party and friends were to arrive a day early to water ski, swim, boat and picnic at Birch Lake on Friday, July 3. By the hundreds they came, pouring into Bartlesville from across the country for the wedding of the century when Mike would appear just in time for his wedding—or so some believed and many hoped.

Again, Lenore watched the activities as though peering through hazy lenses, straining to see the meaning of her wedding weekend without Mike at her side. On Saturday night, Lenore with some close friends piled into a pick-up truck and drove to a big field to set off fireworks, just as planned earlier. "We cried—and laughed—through the night," she said. Never had fireworks for the Fourth moved the cluster of friends more deeply.

"God even cried on my wedding day," Lenore said. "It thundered and rained hard. But God gave me wonderful grace to soar above the storm like an eagle . . . " When a butterfly landed on her shoulder, she saw it as a symbol of promise, of life. She had lived through the hardest day in her life—"the day I didn't marry Mike."

*****

The following day, incredulity mounted as nearly a thousand friends and family gathered in Mike's home church, not for a wedding, but for a memorial service. Dr. C. B. Colaw, whose marriage had been performed by Mike's grandfather fifty years earlier, and who himself had assisted in the wedding of Mike's parents thirty years earlier, prayed these words written by Harold McEwan:

> You are the light that never goes out, the ear that is never shut, the eye that is never closed, the mind that never gives up, the heart that never grows cold, the hand that never stops reaching, the tongue that never slips, and the love that never fails . . . When we have you, we are conscious of a joy unspeakable . . . a deep settled peace; a precious hiding place; a shelter in the time of storm . . . When we have you, defeat can be turned into victory, frustration transformed to confidence, and uncertainty to assurance.

Then reverently, more than 900 voices lifted praise to the God of their high moments, the God of their deepest need. Most knew and lived the words, but many had never before been put to the test as they were at that moment. Tears flowed freely. The color guard stood at attention. Piano, organ and people swelled as one instrument. "Bless the Lord, O my soul, and all that is within me bless his holy name . . ."

One by one, they spoke of Mike. His sister Denise closed the eulogies by reading a letter she would have written to Mike on May 19, had she known what the next day held for him, and for her. Thanking him for letting her be his tomboy sister, she reminded him that life would have been easier without him. "Do you realize what a hard act you are to follow?" she asked her brother.

Mike's older sister Nadean poured her pain into her violin solo in tribute to Mike and to her God. Don and Naomi courageously spoke. People responded to Pastor Jimmy Johnson's invitation to those who were not already believers to come to Christ. That's just what Mike would have wanted.

The service was over. Mike had not appeared. Then the minister announced that the Mueller family would precede the others from the service, adding, "Oh, Lenore, you can go too." Not only would she not lead them on Mike's arm in the recessional, but also her unique position intensified her shredded emotions. "It was my wedding weekend, but because of Mike's assumed death, I suddenly became an afterthought," she said.

The anonymous poem, *High Flight*, printed in the Order of Worship, might have been Mike's message to Lenore.

Oh, I have slipped the surly bonds of earth
and danced the skies on laughter-silvered wings.
Sunward I've climbed, and joined the tumbling mirth
of sun-split clouds and done a hundred
things you have not dreamed of.

Wheeled and soared and swung high

in the sunlit silence. Hov'ring there,
I've chased the shouting wind along
and flung my eager craft through
footless halls of air.

Up, up the long, delirious, burning blue,
I've topped the windswept heights with easy grace
where never lark, or even eagle flew.
And, while with silent, lifting mind I've trod
the high untrespassed sanctity of space,
I put out my hand and touched the face of God.

That night after the service, still teetering between believing he was alive and knowing he might not return, Lenore gave Mike's Naval Academy pocketwatch to his friend Alan. She left Bartlesville, but not for a honeymoon. Through the long, hot summer, Christmas and Easter of 1988, Lenore continued to pray and hope, write to friends and in her journal.

Hiding much of her anger and depression behind the public facade, she still knew only one certainty: Mike was missing. Excerpts from journals and letters revealed both pain and victory.

> "It doesn't get any easier. I wonder if it ever will, if I'll ever again have meaning or purpose in life. I love Mike so much. I need him. I hope and pray that if God doesn't allow Mike to come home, that I'll learn how to live on. Right now, I don't know how . . . O, for God to let this nightmare end. If Mike's alive, I need him. He needs us. If he's not alive, I need to say goodbye . . ."
>
> "I'm looking forward to school, to science, to scuba diving—to life. I reach into the depths of my soul in search of purpose to sustain me one more day . . . I believe it is my call, my duty, to believe 100 percent that my husband is alive and well . . . Today, God has granted me a beautiful peace. I have wonderful memories in my head, as well as thoughts of wonderful times to come. Right now, it is beyond my capability even to imagine Michael not coming

home . . . I've chosen not to allow my emotions to interfere with my faith. I look forward to walking through a long aisle of Swordsmen!"

Sometimes a growing realization terrified her. If Mike was still alive, he must be going through hell. Twisting the gold wedding band around and around on her finger, she was afraid that if she removed it, Mike wouldn't return. Waiting through her own advent, pregnant only with ongoing hope, Lenore sometimes wished she were carrying Mike's child. She longed for more than memories and dreams; she wanted more than old letters and pictures to absorb her thoughts and energies; she wanted a warm body to hold and to love.

The severe mercy of some friends—and even strangers —kept her balancing on a tightrope that stretched high above her chasm of doubt. Some confirmed without a doubt, that Mike, at least, was alive. Their visions and signs, dreams and clairvoyance, gave shape and substance to Lenore's image of returning to Bartlesville—next time with Mike.

The voices of four women of Bartlesville began as a phantom whisper. Growing bolder, by the end of that year they shouted what the Navy, and even the families and I could no longer believe. How could these women possibly hang onto the assurance that Mike had survived?

I would ask them myself. I packed again for Bartlesville.

CHAPTER 5

BELIEVING THE IMPOSSIBLE

[God] brought them out of darkness
and the shadow of death . . .
—Psalm 107:13 (KJV)

Esther Snyman opened her home to me in Bartlesville. Early on the morning after my arrival, I drove to Mike's home and parked in the space across the street where cottonwood trees spread downhill to shade the winding Pathfinder Trail. Here the Marines from Broken Arrow Marine base had also parked on the evening they entered the Mueller house with life-changing news.

Part of the essence of hope is looking for ways to sustain itself. And some of the impetus to believe that Mike had survived a crash grew from a vigorous source of hope: the Christian clairvoyants. They combined their gift of discernment with prayers and offers to help find the missing men. Difficult to ignore, they affirmed continually and resolutely: Mike is alive.

At first, their news encouraged the family. The rumors tantalized all of us who loved him. It wasn't as though the four women clairvoyants had *evidence*, but neither did the Navy have *evidence* to the contrary. They stood on common ground:

The men and the F-18 Hornet were still missing. One group said they were *dead*. The other group said they were *alive*. So, while Don and Naomi resisted both claims, we all prayed the Christian discerners were right. Connie called first. Then Betty. Then other discerners—a more palatable name than *psychics* or *clairvoyants* for the Christian community—joined them. Ann reported seeing visions that assured her Mike was coming home and that they would hear something definitive within 24 hours. But they waited on.

Bertha, too, talked about her visions. She always saw Mike alive, but disoriented. One day she saw someone carrying Mike on his back. "They will arrive at sunset," she said. "The sky will be red. . . " But the sun set, and rose, and set again, as we waited.

Don and Naomi trusted God and the scriptures. Their strong beliefs based on scripture and church tradition pricked Don and Naomi for even considering the preposterous notions of the women. Two other realities, however, jammed total rejection of their claims. First, Connie and Betty are Christian women. Believers. They pray, study the Bible, attend church and acknowledge their clairvoyance as God's gift. Moreover, Mike was still missing. But Don was especially troubled by their claims. Conscientious beyond reproach, Don wrestled with the conflict between his trust in a sovereign God and the hope that these Christian women offered them. "We don't seek out these women—they come to us, over and over again. They pray. They tell us their faith and knowledge. They ask God for the truth to come out in God's time," Don said.

"We never asked for their help, and we wish we hadn't received it," Naomi acknowledged. "Some people ask us how a Christian can delve into that kind of thing. We do not! We are criticized even for talking to the women when they call us. Connie believes her ability is a gift from God. She knows—she is absolutely convinced—that Mike is coming back. Can you understand why . . ."

Naomi gestured helplessly when her voice broke.

Through a torrent of tears she continued, "We would never choose anything that is not God's will. We would never contact a worldly psychic—or even a Christian one."

Struggling for control, she reiterated the obvious. But hearing her, its powerful simplicity shook me: "When they tell us they are sure Mike is alive, I want to believe them." From the counter where I sat with my notes and recorder, I could barely see Naomi's spotless kitchen through my own tears. Well, of course this mother wanted to believe them. It would be easier for the Navy—and the church and families—if everyone accepted that two sons and brothers, one a fiance, one a husband and father, were dead. But to these women, Mike was on his way home.

"Just what if—" Naomi pushed a box of tissues closer to me and tried again. "What if they are right?" She brightened considerably. "God works in mysterious ways!" She quoted scriptures as easily as she played the grand piano in her parlor. Surely God is not confined by ways and means dictated by humans. In their Christian gentility, Don and Naomi did not ask the women to stop calling.

"You'll want to meet Connie," Naomi interjected abruptly. "Her father drew pictures of the people who captured Mike." Pictures? Captured Mike? Had I missed something? "You'll want to see Betty, too," Naomi rushed on. "She worked with the St. Louis Police to find missing children. She knows Mike is alive, too."

Other interviews could wait. I had to meet these persons who were so sure Mike was alive. I savored those words: *Mike is alive.* I rolled them over and over in my mind like a morsel of rich milk chocolate melting in my mouth. Feeling it. Tasting it. Wanting it to last forever. Letting it become part of me. Alive . . . alive . . . alive . . .

* * * * *

Connie had a lot of experience in psychic phenomena, in

spite of her thirtyish look. As a child, she didn't know that prescience was unusual. She gave her parents information they learned to trust. "Someone will come in a red car today," she once announced. Sure enough, someone did. As young as ten, Connie helped police locate a missing person. She revealed the pain and risk that sometimes accompany her perceptions, making her afraid to use the gift, such as the time she became aware that a man seated in front of her had a brain tumor.

"The mind interprets the vision from out of personal experience," she explained. She fears most that she'll misinterpret a vision. Working with Randy, a hypnotist, Connie held Mike's boyhood picture while describing him playing baseball. She moved on, finally sensing the F-18 where she observed Dan and Mike looking at a map. She struggled to see the name of one spot: *CAN—KAV—KAD*.

After one vision she feared something terrible had happened to Mike. "I don't know how to tell you this," she told Don. She believed Dan Ginsberg had been hurt seriously when they impacted, and that he lived for about two days. But she had seen Mike in a place with huge rocks. His compass didn't work, so he was wandering in a maze-like area. In another vision she saw a black box in the hot, sandy terrain. In another, she thought she saw Jesus, but it was Mike, his beard and hair long and shaggy. He was weak, sick, asking her to pray for him.

Much of what Connie said included perceptual sensory descriptions and the words, *feel, feeling*. I wanted something ordinary, tangible, familiar. I listened to the refrigerator hum quietly in the background and sipped on water.

Of course, we are spirit. We are far more than physical bodies. We understand so little of the miracle of life, of the mind and spirit and soul. Could this be authentic in the sense that she was *feeling* the vibrations of a human being half a continent away whose mind was all he had to communicate with?

"I don't know," Connie interrupted my wandering thoughts, "if these were just feelings. I just don't know." So, she didn't know either.

When she began dreaming the same scene every night, she asked her father, an artist, to sketch her perceptions. She prayed he would not create, but rather that God would help him to "see" the four men and a woman through her descriptions. She confirmed that his renderings were accurate representations of the people she believed had found Mike and were using him in their drug trade.

"I'm not trying to prolong this. As soon as they have positive identification, I'll believe it," Connie said. "If Mike is gone, that's it. But the Lord hasn't told us that yet. Well—I've probably bored you long enough," Connie stopped abruptly. She gave me a sad, unfinished-business look. We could talk forever, but that wouldn't change anything.

"Well," I responded, "you've hardly bored me. Maybe confused me. But definitely not bored me!" I thanked her for her time and requested her father's drawings. But she questioned me further. "Well, what have I confused you on?" I didn't know where to begin.

"No one thing," I told her. "I'm just super-saturated. I see so many conflicts, have many questions, sense much confusion." Oops. That word again. I had to get away. I had to make sense of something when I understood nothing.

That night I examined Connie's father's realistic drawings of the drug ring she believed had captured Mike in the wilderness. "Mike's being used," Connie had concluded. I shivered and began to read into the night, begging God for—I knew not what . . .

* * * * *

The next day I drove to Betty's house. She first heard that Mike was missing while taking organ lessons from Mike's Aunt Cara Lee in May, 1987. She soon received the same impression as Connie: Mike had been captured by drug runners. Connie and Betty had neither met nor discussed that idea with anyone.

For six years she had studied psychic phenomena and worked with police in St. Louis to locate missing children. "Could you tell me, Betty, if the plane and the bodies are discovered, how might you explain your impressions?"

"Well it's a gift, right?" she replied with a question of her own.

"But," I pushed her, "what if the proof is definitive? Let's say they find bodies and identify them through dental records, blood types, DNA testing. That would indicate that your impressions are mistaken."

"Well," she said, "I can miss—in two other cases I missed." She went on to describe a series of fascinating examples of both successes and failures in her work. When the police asked her to talk to the parents of one missing child, the first thing the father told her was, "If you say one thing against this Bible, you're off this case."

"Well," Betty quickly interjected, "I'm not against the Bible. In fact, I'm a Christian. He was afraid he'd offend God, yet he wanted desperately to find his son. I worked on this case just after Mike disappeared." She stopped to locate a picture. It confirmed the worst for the missing child. "The parents didn't want to believe it, but the police found him, just as I'd told them."

"And you feel just as strongly that Mike is alive?" I asked.

"Yes, he was trying to get away."

"Away from what?"

"Away from the people who captured him."

"Captured him? How was he found? How did they take Mike?"

"Well, I think they watched for planes, and shot him down . . . "

I felt she'd shot *me* down. After all, it wasn't a balloon she was talking about. I had wanted to believe—again—in the possibility that Mike was alive when Betty interjected the preposterous idea of civilians watching for and shooting down an F-18 in the Sierra Nevada.

"But here—come with me." Her sudden interruption catapulted me back into the room. "I'll show you a little of how it works," she said. What was I getting myself into, anyway? She took me into a small room with a card table set up in the center. Taking one chair, she motioned me to take the other across from her. Picking up a deck of cards, she handed them to me and told me to shuffle them. I had never perfected the art even when playing *Fish* or *Rook* with the children. I hadn't grown up playing cards, but she needed for me to handle them to be able to read me. It was foreign to me. But after all, this was part of my search for Mike. I finished fumbling and handed them to her.

She told me I would have a visitor from my childhood soon, and that my husband and I needed money for something—but doesn't everyone? The afternoon brightness had faded into shadow. I heard her husband return to the house. Exhaustion sapped my ability to reason. The day had filled me with every imaginable emotion. I couldn't wait to return to Esther's.

* * * * *

Mike's sister Denise knew about these women discerners of Bartlesville. She trusted Connie's sincerity and her faith in God, but her faith was not in Connie. Her sister Nadean was troubled about the accusations directed toward her parents. "That hurts me a lot," she confided. "They say it's wrong to listen to anyone who says they have gifts of perception, but someone who never went through this can't fully understand."

"If the discerners' insistence on Mike's survival is upsetting you, that is cruel," I later told Naomi. "No, I just appreciate their efforts," she responded. "They're not getting anything out of it except criticism. Connie prays God will reveal it to her when she is not perceiving things accurately. The women respect our privacy and concerns. It's hard on them—physical, emotional, spiritual energy goes into their work."

While some of their claims seemed too far-fetched to consider, so did the constantly confusing information the military community provided. That Betty and Connie, Bertha and Ann and others would feed the family hope, angered some, encouraged others, and disturbed all of us. But believing that Mike was alive compelled the women to reveal what they "knew" before it was too late.

Their discernment may well be a gift. Of course, the gift can be misused. Or misinterpreted. Or simply, but terribly, mistaken. But as I drove back to Esther's, I felt foolish to admit even to myself: *It could also be right.*

* * * * *

Lenore, too, hung on to thin threads of hope, grasping every one thrown to her by friends—and even strangers—waiting for rescue from her own disappearance from reality. Friends related incredible true stories about pilots who crashed and appeared months later. Lenore wrote in her journal about scores of signs, dreams and visions that encouraged her to believe that Mike, at least, had survived.

Such persons as Roy Martin, the official artist of the Air Force, astronaut Jim Irwin, the Joint Chiefs of Staff at the Pentagon, and hundreds of other Christians wrote of their prayers. Others offered such words of hope as these: "In just one month they'll return." Or, "They will return tomorrow." Or, "Mike and Dan will walk out . . . "

Strange sensory perceptions intensified Lenore's hopes. One night while sleeping she felt very warm, so she sent her warmth to Mike and felt chills the rest of the night . When she tasted berries in the milk, she knew Mike was eating berries; when she noticed a strong fish odor, she believed Mike was eating fish. Sleeping in Mike's flight suit, she was poked in the arm and awoke feeling Mike had hurt his arm. She talked to him and "sent" him her strength.

Supernatural occurrences encouraged her. One man said, "God told me Mike is alive." He prayed God would send Lenore an angel. Perfect peace enveloped her when a gold triangle floated across the room. One day a voice startled Lenore, saying, *How could you give up on me?* But such obsessive thoughts made her feel Mike's survival was her responsibility.

When the dress shop would not take back her wedding dress, Lenore wanted to believe that meant she would wear it. As Mike's plane ticket to the wedding was non-refundable, even under such circumstances, she continually questioned: *Could there be a reason? Are these signs that he is alive?* Many signs included colors, specific words, songs, or books, such as *The Hobbit*, in which the hobbit discovered his possessions being auctioned off because everyone thought he was dead.

Naomi also hung on, sometimes tentatively, sometimes resolutely. The pastor of a United Methodist Church Mike had attended announced he had asked God to spare his congregation from loss of life due to military accidents when he arrived eight years earlier. In six weeks he would move; no tragedies marred the record. Naomi's pastor and others affirmed their belief that *with God all things are possible.* "We didn't *know* that Mike was gone, so I began to hope for the miracle," she said. When Naomi read from Psalm 107:4-7, she saw it as a clue: "They cried unto the Lord in their trouble, and he delivered them out of their distresses. God led them forth by the right way, that they might go to a city of habitation . . . God brought them out of darkness and the shadow of death . . ." Her excitement soared. "They *could* walk out! God *could* bring them to a city!" Naomi reasoned she shouldn't give up so easily by accepting Mike's death.

"Maybe God wants to give my faith a workout," she said. Lenore also looked to the scriptures that seemed to confirm her faith in Mike's return, such as her mother's devotional reading from Hebrews 10:37-38: ". . . in just a very little while, he who is coming will come and will not delay."

These moments of believing the men would be found alive contrasted with the depths of despair they experienced at other times. Sorting through these lifelines seemed as fruitless as sorting through an assortment of ropes to save a drowning child. Naomi, Lenore and others hung on to each one to use as needed. They were not ready to give up on Mike, while Marilyn had accepted that her husband would not come home.

I had listened to women discerners who have their own ways of searching. I had heard testimonies of visions, dreams and signs to perpetuate the preposterous claims that Mike was alive.

The Navy dismissed it all. But my search differed from that of the Navy: While they searched for a body, I searched for a person.

CHAPTER 6

GROWING UP MUELLER

A wise son brings joy to his father,
but a foolish son grief to his mother.
—Proverbs 10:1

Even a child is known by his actions . . .
—Proverbs 20:11a

Before leaving Bartlesville I needed to explore what it's like to grow up *Mueller.* Don had left early in his red and white pick-up truck. A building contractor in Bartlesville, he is known for honesty and punctuality. Naomi teaches music and plays piano at First Wesleyan Church. She can quote more scripture than a Southern Baptist evangelist. But it's not the quoting that gets you; it's the way she's lived it during these gut-wrenching years.

We walked through the den past Don's comfy recliner and Mike's oversize graduation picture. Crisp and serious, the United States Naval Academy officer looked down at us, undisturbed by our conversation about his disappearance a year earlier. A vivid fuschia gloxinia, given by Esther on the first anniversary of the news, cascaded over a pot in one corner of the den.

Sitting on Mike's bed we looked through albums, scrapbooks and Navy memorabilia. He'd always dreamed of flying, interspersed with typical boyhood aspirations: a fireman, a doctor, a baseball player. Don and Naomi centered their children's upbringing in spiritual development. As early as he talked, he prayed daily for "eggiebuggie." Hearing Bible stories from birth, Mike could answer questions about the characters even as a toddler. Once when asked what Lot's wife turned into, he spoke up knowingly, "Pepper and salt!" At 3 1/2, he sang his first solo in church. One morning when Don read the story of David and Goliath, Mike began quoting it—and he never stopped quoting scripture.

Mike's parents pray specifically for each child by name every Sunday evening, recognizing that even the most conscientious parents can't discern what is best for each child in every situation, but that God gives wisdom for difficult times. One time Mike's strong will needed tempering. After being disciplined, he angrily and stubbornly determined not to cry. Mike's hardness frightened Naomi. She poured out her feelings to him, telling him she wanted him to be a man of God. He softened, and they prayed together, cried and hugged.

"If I hadn't won in that situation," she figured, "it would have been more difficult for Mike to submit to God's authority. That was a turning point, a definite breakthrough." A second spiritual breakthrough followed the accident that nearly took his eyesight. Navy/Marine aviators must have perfect vision to land on carriers at sea. Each time he passed a physical, Mike exulted over his excellent eyesight as though it were a miracle. It was. I would hear that whole story later. Mike saw that trauma as a test with God asking: *Are you willing to fly—or not to fly—whichever is in my will?*

Naomi will always remember his response: "If I never get to the Academy, or fly for the Navy, then God has a better idea."

In a missions convention during his elementary years,

Mike responded to the appeal for faith pledges. While the girls each pledged about $50 for the year, Mike pledged $200—as much as he had made the whole previous year by working for a dollar an hour for Don in the summer. Aghast, Naomi questioned his wisdom, but he replied, "Mom, the man said it was a *faith* pledge"—and sure enough, he fulfilled it.

Mike supported his flying habit once he earned his pilot's license in high school with a variety of jobs including cleaning carpets with his own shampooer. By age fourteen, he assumed payments on a house, paid closing costs and taxes, kept records, did upkeep and interviewed prospective renters. By the time he was 16, he owned a second house.

Sometimes his mother thought, *This kid is not for real*. She began to speak with difficulty through her tears, as she continued to reveal her son's character through a mother's memory. If I hadn't known Mike, I'd have chalked up Naomi's accolades to a grieving mother's imagination.

Sometimes he struggled with how to witness to acquaintances and strangers about his relationship with God. He wasn't into witnessing on street corners, but instead witnessed by the way he lived. While company commander, he got up even earlier on Friday mornings to cook the weekly prayer breakfast for youth at the church he attended. Buddies teased him for drinking Coke rather than beers, but no one denied that Mike knew how to party.

His prayer diary showed his reliance on God. He believed resolutely that God was working things out for his good, even when things didn't go his way. When he missed his flight home for Christmas break in his Plebe year and spent the next 24 hours in the airport, he responded: *God has something to teach me.*

Naomi committed herself to encouraging the children to excel. "Parents often think their kids' activities are life-threatening," she said, "so they worry and fret, or try to control everything they do. But Psalm 112:7 says: *[She] will not be afraid of bad news. [Her] heart is fixed, trusting in the Lord.*"

Mike wrote to adults just to keep in touch, and often acknowledged their contribution to his life, endearing him to people of every age. In each letter Mike told his family and friends he loved them, and even thanked them for the littlest things. Naomi began to laugh through her tears. "He'd write: *Thanks for your love or prayers, or for my training—and for the stamps!* Apparently they don't sell stamps at the Academy!"

Just then, the telephone rang. Both of Mike's sisters were planning a trip home. Denise and Mike were only 13 months apart and Nadean was 2 1/2 years older. Mike idolized Nadean, and in Denise, he had a buddy.

* * * * *

Don had his own stories to tell when he stopped in for a generous lunch Naomi prepared seemingly without effort. He reminisced about Mike in his quietly reserved way, reminding me of the strong but gentle carpenter of nearly 2000 years ago on whose life and teachings the family patterned all they did.

He began by recalling Mike's birth in Colorado Springs, Colorado. While living in Kansas, already attracted to machinery, Mike climbed in the car, pulled it out of gear, and rode it down the driveway incline, across the street and curb, and into an open lot— quite an adventure for a three-year-old tyke—and his parents.

They moved to Bartlesville when Mike was five and Don joined his brother in the contracting business. Soon, Mike wanted to work for money. Often working side-by-side, Don and Mike spent more time together than many fathers and sons. When Mike and his friends worked on a house, Don often told them, "If you can work and talk, that's fine. But if not, get about ten feet apart and just work!"

Don wore his pride in Mike humbly. He didn't seem to realize that his son learned to be a conscientious worker by observing his Dad. But Mike also knew how to balance play and work. He was a 100 percenter, whether relaxing, studying or working. Don couldn't help bragging about Mike's activities as youth group president, participation in singing groups and Bible quiz teams, and as drum major in high school. Proud, of course, when Mike was accepted into the Naval Academy and later became company commander, his gratitude and pride reached its zenith when he heard about Mike's Christian influence there.

Don carried his plate to the sink, just as I'd seen Mike do, rinsed it and put it in the dishwasher. Leaning against it, he folded his brown muscular arms across his broad chest. I can imagine Jesus, were he living on earth today, spending time with Don. Jesus and his disciple, of sterling character and deeply thoughtful, would build houses, and the kingdom, together.

Don called me into the den where he showed me check stubs and other precious collections that represented Mike, loud and clear, even in the silence. "If you look at your checkbook," Don said, "you'll see where your priorities are." Mike's check register from boyhood days showed payments to his friends who worked for him in his businesses, gifts for missions, and always his regular weekly check to pay a tithe of his earnings to the church.

Then Don picked up a small, plastic-wrapped package. Reverently removing its contents, he handed me a worn, gray cardboard composition book. I opened it carefully. Mike's familiar, tiny, neat print filled its pages. " . . . you're the God of the living, not the dead. Help me to be alive in you and show others your message. Let me love you above all others with all my heart, soul, mind, and strength! You are truly awesome!"

"These things don't just happen, Don," I said when I found my voice. "You and Naomi lived as examples to Mike, so he became who he was. Perhaps he was a remarkable boy and young man, but your teaching and example provided the pattern."

"But most kids don't live like Mike even if their parents are similar examples," Don explained. "His devotional record amazed us. I had no idea he wrote his own personal communion with God . . . " Shaking his head, Don quietly walked toward the kitchen door. I couldn't see his face, but I heard the pain in his retreating voice. The front door opened and closed. Several minutes later I heard his truck start and pull away.

* * * * *

Mike had an unusual commitment to encouraging his parents. Several quotes from letters that Don and Naomi generously opened to me showed that sensitivity and expressive love.

To his dad he wrote:

> I hope your houses are moving along and you're keeping busy . . . I am definitely not jealous of your being a builder. To me, that seems more risky than being a fighter pilot. I guess to each his own, huh? Hopefully, I can help you again one of these days because I enjoy working for you. You're a great employer as well as father . . . you have been, are, and always will be a great dad. Thanks so much for all you've done for me and all you've taught me.

In another he wrote:

> I just can't thank God enough for such terrific parents. I know I wouldn't be flying jets today if you hadn't encouraged me since kid-hood. You really are terrific and complement each other beautifully. Thanks for being such a great example! I think we have an AWESOME family!

Sensitive to their feelings, Mike wrote this to his mom after a disagreement:

> I am truly sorry if I upset you last night by my hasty

actions. I just want you to know I appreciate your genuine concern for my spiritual life, dating life, and life in general! I love you a lot. Thanks so much for all you did over break: my wash, the stamps, the moral support—and sermons!

Whereas most kids ask for the car when they come home for break, he wrote:

Do you think we could fly the 206 up to Wichita? I'll even pay for half—can't beat that, huh!?

Sending pictures, he told them:

They can be circulated to any eligible young woman—you know the requirements. We don't settle for just anything, but still love them all. Remember, when the time comes, she'll be your daughter-in-law for life and the mother of your grandkids. Heavy, huh?!

Growing up *Mueller* also included an uncountable extended family. In her nineties, Mike's Grandma Ireland lived downstairs in the Mueller household in her own apartment. When Naomi told her Mike's plane was missing, she responded, "I knew that." She had seen the Marine truck bring the messengers who reported Mike's disappearance.

One of 12 children, Don was about seven years old when the railroad station operator delivered a telegram to his parents near the close of World War II: Don's brother Dave was missing. Of twelve children and forty grandchildren, first a son, and then a grandson, had disappeared in military service.

* * * * *

A graphic artist working in Tulsa, Denise had driven up to Bartlesville to talk with me about her missing brother. You'd think at the Mueller house, people would be guarded in talking about Mike. Instead, everyone thinks and talks about

Mike continuously. A tomboy, Denise loved to hang out with Mike and his friends. They played sports and were generally "the bad guys." She doesn't recall ever talking with Mike seriously, but they played and laughed plenty. Crushed by never having let Mike know how much he meant to her, she has determined to tell people she loves them, not to hold grudges, and to share Christ with others.

Still learning to view circumstances from God's perspective, Denise wrote to Alan after Mike disappeared, describing her journey of faith. Believing him to be alive, she realized that God couldn't have chosen a better person than Mike to stand up under the testing he was undoubtedly experiencing. "Rather than giving in to anger and bitterness that often plague me when I think about Mike," she explained, "instead I choose faith and acceptance . . . that gives me a whole new freedom, knowing that no matter what the circumstance is, I can choose joy."

* * * * *

Mike's older sister Nadean carried her violin with her everywhere. She would never leave it in the car with other luggage when traveling. She practiced faithfully each day, but when strains of Bach or Vivaldi flowed under the doors and through the walls into my soul, it didn't sound like practicing to me.

At first, Nadean had a hard time getting into the feelings. Sometimes, starting far enough back from an event so catastrophic as Mike's disappearance gives the lover-left-behind a running start, so that by the time he or she gets up to the feeling point, the story is flowing. Eventually, disjointed thoughts wove themselves into one more love story.

"Mike was genuine, not a people-pleaser," Nadean described him. "He neither allowed people to control him, nor did he control them. He was no less an object person than a people person. Most guys who get a bread mixer for a wedding gift wait until married to open the box. But not Mike! In no time, he was making bread, calling himself the flying baker."

Nadean tried to tell me about the video camera. Crying, she could scarcely talk, so instead she handed me a letter from Mike that suggested purchasing a video camera for their parents' Christmas gift. "But we couldn't wait for Christmas," Nadean said, "so on Mike's first Thanksgiving at home in years, and later during Christmas, we took so many videos. Were they our last of Mike at home?" she mused.

Looking into Nadean's tear-filled eyes, I felt like a trespasser into her soul. Even with the support of others, her anguish was still her anguish, her pain, her cross. We talked about experiencing grief as individuals, each expressing it uniquely. While Denise wrote long letters to friends, Naomi talked freely about Mike, and Don wrote private journals, Nadean communicated her feelings through music.

After hearing that Mike had disappeared, Nadean played in a scheduled trio concert that evening, even though her performance had suddenly become totally insignificant.

"On the slow, expressive movements, I literally cried through the medium of music," she recalled. "My heart bled into every note. Never before had I experienced that depth of emotion, deep sadness and pain. That first week was the longest in my life."

Through her tears, Nadean read from her journal written after the news: "This has made me re-evaluate my priorities. Auditions and concerts don't have the importance they had. Who cares? They seem so small and insignificant." *Who cares?* expressed Nadean's feelings not only about the violin, but also about everything for a time.

The words of Jim Elliot, martyred in the fifties as a young missionary pilot, remind her of Mike: *"Wherever you are, be all there. Live to the hilt every situation you believe to be the will of God."*

That was Mike. In fact, the whole Mueller-Ireland clan

lives this way. Their commitment to God and the Church, to work and play, to family and friends, to mission and service, invades every cell of their being. They live intentionally, never by default. They believe that to die is gain, that death is the anesthetic from which we awaken to live forever in God's presence.

That's what it's like to grow up *Mueller* in Bartlesville. But, I needed to move beyond Mike's family, to discover both Mike's impact on a community and its influence on him.

CHAPTER 7

BARTLESVILLE

. . . they found him in the temple courts,
sitting among the teachers,
listening to them and asking them questions . . .
When his parents saw him, they were astonished . . .
—Luke 2:46, 48

Sky hangs like a giant canopy over Bartlesville. Oil well pumps perch like giant insects over parched flat countryside and in lush, watered back yards. Community pride and institutions cherish and maintain the historical landmarks like the old Foster Mansion, the Frank Phillips Home and the 1898 Dewey Hotel. Visitors can't forget where they are when they see the *Sooners* hailed everywhere. Embodying the ideals of sound family life and wholesome patriotism, its 37,000 residents welcome visitors to its open gateway to the past Old West and the New Southwest.

Bartlesville townspeople cycle and jog on the winding 11-mile Pathfinder Parkway. They enjoy concerts and drama in the $13 million Bartlesville Community Center and Price Tower designed by Frank Lloyd Wright. They fish, hunt and go boating in the abundant waters and timberlands of northeast Oklahoma.

The Bartlesville Symphony, Civic Ballet, Little Theater, Bartlesville Choral Society and Bartlesville Art Association provide cultural enrichment. The influence of the Phillips family oil empire dominates the landmarks: the original Frank Phillips building and tower; the old train station, now restored and housing the Chamber of Commerce offices; the impressive Hotel Phillips where Mike and Lenore had secret reservations for the honeymoon suite; the Phillips mansion; the Jane Phillips Hospital; and Phillips Boulevard.

History shakes its bones and comes to life in museums like Woolaroc and Tom Mix; in names like the James brothers, Will Rogers, and Nellie Johnstone; in Native American lore from the Osage, Delaware, and Cherokee tribes; in early traders like Nelson Carr and Jacob H. Bartles, after whom the town was named and incorporated in 1875.

One evening just before dusk, I settled into the back seat while Don and Naomi narrated a tour of their All-America City. Naomi pointed out the Nellie Johnstone No. 1, Oklahoma's first commercial oil well (1875) in the park by the same name. Watching a child play there, I imagined Mike climbing on the ferris wheel years earlier, then racing to the kids' roller coaster, then on to the miniature train. Several miles later, we passed Sooner Park where children still play, and where Mike first practiced riding a motorcycle.

Next up was the Bartlesville airport. "This is where Mike parked his car," Don said pensively. "And where he started flying," Naomi added. On a flat, quiet little field, a few piper cubs were scattered like toys in a little boy's back yard. Once Mike requested a plane and personnel wouldn't allow it. They weren't sure he qualified. A friend told him, "You ought to buzz them with your jet sometime." Not knowing Mike had stopped in Tempe, Arizona, to take his FAA rating exam on his way to Lemoore, his parents were surprised to receive the results after Mike disappeared: 110 percent. We gazed across the field where Mike had started his nearly ten-year flying career. No activity. Just Oklahoma spring quiet.

Don started the engine and pulled away. I swatted at the *if only* gnat of a thought that plagued me and tuned in to the tour guides again. Don pointed out College High School where Mike had been drum major, and then drove through the picturesque campus of Bartlesville Wesleyan College, not only part of Mike's and Lenore's heritage, but also the place my brother had served as vice-president for development. It was he who had introduced the Muellers into my life.

Many memories, many ghosts rode with us that evening. Suddenly, all was quiet. Darkness tiptoed around us. We stopped talking, laughing, reminiscing. But it was more than being talked out. It was like those magnetic moments at the ocean when you watch the sun slipping inch by inch, lower and lower in the western horizon. Strangely, you don't notice or feel the earth's revolving except in those last minutes when you seem to sense its movement. You lose your train of thought. You catch your breath. You focus on the sun with eyes squinted as if to hold onto it, knowing that once you let it slip away with all the warmth and light and life that sustains you, the night will set in; knowing that when the last sliver of orange or crimson disappears, a little of your life drops over the edge with it.

Don and Naomi dropped me off at Esther's after our tour. She greeted us tearfully because she was viewing the video of the California memorial service for Mike. It had stirred smoldering memories of her husband's illness and death years earlier. A few months after the diagnosis, Niko had died of cancer when he was 44, leaving Esther with two young children. In unsuspecting moments, a glance, a picture, a sound, a smell, a touch in a dream sometimes still ignited a flame that burned and hurt again.

Talking about Mike triggered a long-ago dream that she related: When one of her children answered the ringing phone one night after Niko's death, Esther realized it was Niko. She waited, ecstatic, wrapped in superlative anticipation for her turn. Finally, she reached for the phone from the excited youngsters. Breathless with joy, she took the receiver into her hands and exclaimed "NIKO!" But all she heard was a click and a dial tone. She awoke to the sound of her own sobs, one more life-line severed. So it was that Esther understood. She helped me think through details in painful—and often funny—discussions each night, all the while re-living her own personal loss.

It was 3:30 A.M., not a night for sleeping. Sitting on the floor, I plowed through stacks of Mike's papers, letters, pictures, data, documents that Naomi and Don had given me to read. I discovered a postcard from Esther's son Eugene:

> . . . Mom keeps me posted on the situation out in Lemoore. I'm expecting some news soon. It is so natural to anticipate a rendezvous in Colorado with Mike for a ski-week. I don't know whether I miss him more when I think of our history or our future. Throughout there is God, the ever-present Rock: in calm waters or tempest, there God is . . .

Gene would arrive in a few days to reveal another side of Mike.

Before talking with those around town who knew Mike, I wanted to observe the community through my own eyes. I left the house early and headed through the flat countryside to nearby Woolaroc. Osage County abounds with herds of massive humped bison, great white Brahmans, takr goats, llamas, strutting ostriches with crew cuts, white-tailed deer and horned eland. Animals and humans, unafraid of one another in this protected haven, live in peace. Benches looking like ancient rock formations squat among the trees; monuments stand among ancient pin oaks and blooming hibiscus; bird songs fill the silence of the 3600-acre nature trail.

The massive Woolaroc Museum doors of mosaic tile depict native Americans, representing the kinship of all peoples to one another, to Earth, to God. Archeologist Frank Phillips had imported artifacts from South America, including a reposing mummy, as well as exquisite local native American artifacts from 200 to 3000 years past. Paintings, sculpture and weaving outlined an interesting path through early American history, showing the relationship between the pioneers who moved into or through the area and the indigenous native American.

Then, I saw what had kindled longing in Mike in his young years: a life-size replica of a Phillips 66 gas station with an airplane suspended overhead. Yellowed newspapers told the story of an air race and lost planes at sea in 1927 when daredevils attempted to establish air transportation from San Francisco to Honolulu. The Woolaroc, flying with Phillips 66 gas, had made it with enough fuel reserve to fly another 500 miles after its mission.

Dedicated to the boys and girls of today, Woolaroc is also headquarters for the National Y-Indian Guides. Pulling away from the magnetism of that quiet place, I paused to look at the stained glass mural depicting the Indian Guide's Reply that Mike had read:

> ". . . the downhill trail looks easy. But it can lead you into a trap . . .The uphill path is not easy either. It has many risks . . . reach for the stars . . . when you get there, you will feel good—like you have done something big. Then you can guide someone else who doesn't know the way . . . "

Mike had chosen the uphill path. As I drove away, I noticed numerous dirt roads leading off in many directions, but unobtrusive signs directed exiting visitors with two simple words: *This Way*. Just like Mike. Simply and quietly, he became a signpost to all who walked with him, a sign that pointed to Someone and Something higher than himself: *This way . . . this way . . . this way . . .*

* * * * *

I observed Mike's growth into maturity through the memories of those who knew him long before I did. Before he slipped farther from view, I would follow his tracks through Bartlesville.

Mike's retired teacher from Wayside Elementary School, Mrs. Thurlie Tyner, had seen traits in Mike in fourth grade that predicted his success in relationships and profession. "When Mike entered the classroom," she remembered, "it was like the sun coming up."

Another of her students, Donald E. Woolett, like Mike, graduated from the Naval Academy, became a Marine and was engaged to be married when he was killed in the Bierut terrorist bombing.

Driving down Frank Phillips Boulevard I thought about her parting words, "I'll always remember Mike because his ideals were anchored in Someone else." Maybe that's what makes the difference in any young person who dares to live that way: *His ideals were anchored in Someone else.*

Kathy and Hurley Swartz were the Muellers' Farmers Insurance agents. They and their teen-age son Tanen led me into their private office. During Mike's last Christmas break, he had hooked Tanen and other teenage friends with videos and stories about training and the jets he flew. A California native, Kathy told Don and Naomi, "Mike will love the Sierras. You will, too. My Sierras are just wonderful." Now, those words haunt her.

Hurley mourns his missed chance to tell Mike he loved him. "I'll not let that happen again," he said. "The memorial service was one of the saddest experiences of my life. I've lost close friends, but that was just awful. Mike was a *number one* person. Why should someone like that have to go?"

"But, he was so unassuming. No one ever said about him, *Boy, he thinks he is somebody . . .*" Kathy interjected.

"Just by living, by doing usual, everyday living, Mike won more people than most." Hurley hesitated. "If I go on, I'm going to start crying." He readjusted his position and stared hard at his fingernails as I stood to leave.

Alice Ellis was Don's secretary at Mueller Realtors and

Developers. When Mike worked nights for the telephone answering service, he slept there on a couch. In the mornings he'd greet them sleepy-eyed with tousled hair, but never grumpy. He'd fix a cup of hot cocoa and talk awhile before going home to shower and dress for class. "But, you know," she looked around as if ready to let me in on a secret, "I still haven't thrown away his cocoa container. That's just Mike."

When Naomi came to the office one day after Mike disappeared, Alice sensed a strong urge: *Please hug Mom for me*. She thought her boss's wife would think it strange if she suddenly hugged her. But when the impression persisted, she told Naomi, "Someone wants me to hug you."

"I really loved Mike, but I never let him know that," Alice said sadly. "I never want to experience those regrets again. This has changed every relationship. I can never again take for granted the people I care about."

These expressions of love had become commonplace. A boy's life had made a difference in his home town. An American flag, given in memory of Mike, flies above a native limestone structure set on a hill. The people who worship in the First Wesleyan Church there are much like the Muellers: devout and intent in their relationship with God, respectable and honest in their business, joyful and affirming in their association with other people, generous with their means to spread the gospel story and establish churches around the world.

Lori Buck is one of them. Six years old when Mike disappeared, she sat on the floor with me and poured out her heart about Mike. She knew without a doubt that he was alive. She knew he carried her picture with him because, she said, "I saw him open his wallet and put it inside." Adoring him so intently and wanting him back so desperately, the next day she brought the beginnings of a letter in second-grade cursive.

"Dear Mike," she had written, "I wish you wor [sic] here right now. We wood [sic] have fun." She was waiting for Mike's address. Listening to her childlike, uncomplicated faith, hope seeped around the edges of my consciousness.

Wendell and Esther Rovenstine, Mick's parents, met me for lunch at the Chinese restaurant. Mike's last letter to Wendell had requested him to officiate with his pastor at the wedding. Proud of Mick's graduation from the Academy and his flying career, Wendell acknowledged his fascination with comparing Mike and Mick. Mike's disappearance pushed him to great grief and soul searching.

"But my son is *not* Mike," Esther pointed out. "He didn't intend to follow Mike's footsteps. The Academy enhanced opposite qualities in them. For Mike, so confident and accustomed to success, the military discipline and academics rounded off edges of superiority and arrogance. The same disciplines developed impressive leadership skills and self-confidence in Mick who felt he had Mike and older brothers to live up to."

I listened to Esther and Wendell struggle, as all parents do, not only to accept their children for who they are, but also to set them free to be what their temperament leads them to become.

A half-dozen pilots from Bartlesville gave substance to Mike's dream of flying. Mr. Craighead was his first instructor pilot. "You'll never do it that fast," Mr. Craighead advised Mike after hearing his ambitious plan to complete the aviation track at the high school in a very short time. Of course, Mike did. He was 17. Trusting Mike's ability and judgment, Mr. Craighead ruminated over likely causes for a mishap: vertigo, weather, birds, lightning, downdraft, altimeter dysfunction, turbulence . . . on and on the list grew. "How could he just disappear?" he echoed the most repeated question among all the pilots.

Then he moved on from reasoning to reminiscing. Mr. Craighead had written a recommendation for Mike's application to the Academy. It was easy to see that Mr. Craighead hadn't just completed a perfunctory form. His passionate outpouring was an accolade to Mike's character. But he continued, his voice suddenly breaking, coming and going in a crackling sort of way like a radio signal that's fading, "I let them know that when they issued an order to Mike, he would do his utmost to carry it out, and not only that, if he couldn't do it, he'd tell them; and if something was wrong, he'd tell them; and even if one of his buddies did something wrong, he'd still tell them . . ." A retired Air Force colonel, he wrote, "Mike is the kind of man I would want on my staff."

By that time his voice had returned, ending in a powerful crescendo. "They thanked me for taking the time to explain that," he added thoughtfully, "and accepted Mike into the Academy. No one deserved it more than he did."

In Europe when Mike graduated, Mr. Craighead expected to see Mike at the wedding. His face contorted as he struggled with emotion. "But I never saw him again."

Leaving him, I found Bill Mingle, an Air Force pilot-turned-radio announcer who had broadcasted sports when Mike was in high school and college. Though older, Bill was impressed with Mike's self-assurance, his clearly defined purpose and peak physical condition. Bill reminded me that it takes young people like Mike to climb into a high-risk, high performance aircraft.

"It takes men flying off and on aircraft carriers in the middle of the night in the Mediterranean or Pacific; it takes others who go under in the subs and don't see daylight or family for months; it takes others manning a post in Korea or Bosnia in the middle of winter. These sons and daughters, sisters and brothers, husbands and wives belong to us. Not one of them wants to die. They perform not only for personal satisfaction, but also for love of country. Mike was like that," Bill finished passionately.

More than a thousand accidental deaths occur in military, non-combat service every year. "Pilots don't learn to fly an F-18 Hornet by sitting in a chair or a simulator. They don't learn about explosives by reading about them in a book. There are a lot of *Mikes* every day in harm's way," he said. He suggested some causes for mishaps—including *human error*. That notion crept into conversations too often. Being human is not "bad"—but sometimes it does us in.

Having served on Air Force accident investigation boards, Bill had his own idea about Mike and Dan. I wasn't sure I wanted to hear it, but he continued. "Not only do I think there is any way they might have survived, but also, they frequently find no aircraft pieces or human remains."

There. He had thrown me the curve I expected. I hadn't caught it; instead, it hit me squarely in the face. Leaving Bill, I knew he had no doubt that Mike was permanently gone. Driving away I asked myself: *If we could gather everyone together who knows Mike and Dan, including those who searched and those who investigated the mishap, would the majority be weighted in favor of their survival?* I mentally separated them into three groups: those who believed Mike was alive, those who were not sure, and those who knew he was not alive.

I imagined the scene. Identifying those few who stood on my right who believed Mike was still alive did not take too long. Then I watched the gathering of the uncommitted, the still hopeful but increasingly doubtful, who wanted to stand in the middle.

Finally, I envisioned the left side: Certainly most of the military community and probably all pilots, the crowd blurred into one huge mass . . . and I felt a great sadness within me as I joined them. Of course, I also noticed a continual exchange among the groups as many reconsidered the "evidence" of their demise, or dared to hope based on "evidence" of their survival.

I had discovered in Bartlesville the psychics knew a lot about visions, and Mike's family and the townspeople knew a lot about Mike. The town's ambiance as a gateway to the old West and the new had helped to create the man Mike had become. But still missing in the scenario were the closest friends, the inner circle. They would reveal another side of Mike.

CHAPTER 8

THE WIND BENEATH MY WINGS

Greater love has no one than this:
that he lay down his life for his friends.
—John 15:13

Mike had become a living hero. Not through one act, but one day at a time he gave himself away while receiving in like measure from his friends. Mike was neither better nor greater than his companions. Rather, he had integrated something of each friend into himself. At the same time, each friend had *become* Mike in some way—an individual, yet a composite.

Flying with Mike in his late teens tied together the memories of Craig Horton, Ron Brown, Jr., and Scott Slay. They had all flown out of Bartlesville airport with him and testified to Mike's competence and trustworthiness. Mike had befriended Ron in his awkward years, allowing him to grow up around him as a brother. He basked in Mike's acceptance, whether playing at the pool, cleaning the carpets at church, or working with him on a house for Don's construction business. From watching Mike hot-rod his motorcycle to observing him "read the Word" rather than watch too much TV, Ron was fashioning a hero.

Then, Mike took him flying. Much to his joy and surprise,

Ron discovered years later that the same plane he rented to get his own pilot's license was the one Mike had flown to get his license. Doing solo flying now, he finds himself talking to God up there—and talking to Mike. Flying home after he qualified for his pilot's license, he told Mike: *You must be proud of me right now.*

Although a believer since childhood, on the day of Mike's memorial service Ron consciously chose Christianity as a way of life. "That summer was the turning point of my life." Ron gazed at me through tearful eyes. "Mike was my hero. How could my hero die?"

> Did you ever know that you are my hero? . . .
> I would be nothing without you!
> You are the wind beneath my wings.
> —Henley and Silvar

High school friends Jared Bonner and Monte Alexander knew what hero worship was all about. "But I never got to go up with him," Jared said, not hiding his disappointment. Monte relished flying with Mike and recalled sliding into the cockpit on July 5, 1985. "That was my first," he said. "Just the two of us. He let me fly it! We did stalls and heavy turns. I'll never forget it."

"I wanted to be a military pilot, too," Jared admitted, "but now, it doesn't look like I can because of my eyes. Knowing Mike helps me to say it's okay. I'll still be happy—because God has a better idea," he said, echoing Mike's words after a baseball accident threatened his eyesight.

Teaching now at Bartlesville Wesleyan College, Ken Hada credits Mike with his fulfilling his call to ministry. He remembered the baseball incident well. Both Ken and Mike played on the team at BWC. They had asked Terry Hughes to show them some knuckle balls. When someone turned the machine to max, Mike made the nearly fatal mistake of trying to hit one more pitch after he had flipped off his helmet.

The boys gathered around Mike's limp body in helpless

desperation. When Ken thought he saw blood coming from his ear and both eyes swelled shut, they quickly loaded him into a car and raced to the emergency room. "I blew it," Mike said later, thinking his flying days were over.

A favorite memory fills Ken's need to be "with" Mike. After not seeing him for two years, they unexpectedly met in late 1986 on a flight to Houston. They even sat together. Mike's eyes opened wide on take-off. "These babies do some serious climbing!" he exclaimed. Their hour and a half flight to Houston was much too short, but to their surprise, fog rolled in and the airport was closed. They split the cost of a hotel room and shared their *Last Supper* together—Dominoes Pizza and Coke. While Ken felt even then their meeting was providential, six months later he was certain it was.

More than one woman recalled falling in love with Mike. Others may have been too young, but nonetheless cherished the love Mike gave to them. Cheryl Crouch knew Mike through an older brother. While in high school, she visited her brother's college for homecoming one weekend. The parade of gorgeous girls made her feel totally humiliated in her casual pants and a shirt she hadn't even ironed. Finally Mike told her, "Any girl can look beautiful with make-up and the right clothes, but too few figure out that it's what's on the inside that counts. If you have that right, you don't need to worry about anything else."

She regrets never having told Mike what an impact that had on her. "Even now," she said, "when I put on make-up I think of that. He made me feel I was the most important person he knew, a *best friend*—and totally okay."

Hundreds of "best friends" filled Mike's life. "All of us live in a circle of people," Cheryl said thoughtfully. "If we touch only that many, whether it's ten or a hundred, we fill that place uniquely. When that place is empty, life goes on, but no one else can fill that unique place. That makes us all pretty special."

Family was so important to Mike that he made certain he

was "adopted" everywhere he went. Mom was mom, but Mike had a mother at every port that fulfilled his need to belong to family. Edna Ekstrom and her husband Phil met Mike when they became Nadean's Long Island "parents" while at the University of New York. Confessing their earlier heartbreak with their son, Edna admitted their bitterness about young people. Nadean and Mike changed that. The couple began to believe again and now invite students from NY University to their home away from home.

Edna cried as she reminisced about the tender relationship between Mike and Phil. Mike gave Phil a treasured possession inscribed with a personal message. The photograph was taken by Bill Jeffries of Mike flying an A-4 jet, with a magnificent sunburst over the clouds.

When Phil told Mike his neighbor was selling a cycle, Edna wanted to stuff a gag in his mouth. But Mike rode that cycle all the way to Virginia, Florida, Texas, California and, in fact, to Lemoore NAS the morning of May 20. "Isn't it ironic that a motorcycle, not a plane, put me into a tailspin?" Edna asked.

It was almost too much. Too many stories sounded the same—Mike was one incredible guy whose friends outdid one another in halo-polishing. I needed to find a few tarnished—or at least human—spots on the halo. I should have known that Mike himself would lighten up the situation with a touch of his own. I waved goodnight to Don and Naomi after one more day of searching and stepped into the balmy Oklahoma evening. Walking to my car, parked in the by-now-familiar spot across from the Mueller's house, what I saw stunned me. Someone had painted a white streak across my car from the rear tail light to the front fender in one long, ugly sweep with a four-inch paint brush. I glanced around furtively, wondering whether to run back inside. Seeing no one, I jumped in, locked the doors, and headed for Esther's. Who had done it and why? My hands gripped the steering wheel as I pulled into Esther's driveway five minutes later, quivering with tiredness and fear.

Esther followed me outside to check the damage. With my finger I touched a little spot. It was dry. I rubbed one edge—it wasn't even paint! Whitewash? It didn't matter. An innocent prank, it was exactly the kind of thing Mike might have done. In a few minutes we had wiped it clean.

Lighten up! I could hear Mike say, followed by his familiar laugh. When I called Don to see whether they knew of any pranksters in their area, he was surprised. Never before, nor since, had they seen anything like that—not even on Halloween. I wished them a restful night and hung up with a grin.

Was that fun, you crazy guy? How'd you do that? I asked Mike. *You're still up to your old tricks, aren't you? Where are you, anyway? Here? There? Everywhere? Help me out, Mike! Tell me how you did that!*

* * * * *

At last I was to get beyond Mike's sainthood into his mischief. The next day I found Terry Hughes, who teaches in Bartlesville. When Terry moved there about 1972, Mike became his first friend. One overcast day the boys did some fishing at the Jane Phillips Hospital pond. Mike was intense, as he always was about doing things right. They threw out two lines and the fish bit ecstatically. So they put out bobbers all over the pond. Soon they were all popping simultaneously. While Terry raced for one, Mike scampered for another. They were looking for a big bass or a good-looking catfish, but they knew catfish are deep-water fish, and they only had eight-foot lines. Terry threw out a sucker and then forgot about it. When he flopped to the pier to rest, he heard a scream, looked across the pond and saw Mike jumping and yelling, holding a whopper of a catfish over the water—it had to be 8 or 9 pounds.

"Look at this thing!" Mike screamed. Terry yelled back, "Get it on the bank!" No sooner did the fish hear that than it doubled up, the line snapped, and Mike threw a temper tantrum. It was monumental. His face was red. And Mike was left with only a classic story of the fish that got away.

One year at church camp, Terry remembers Mike unpacking three gross of pop bottle rockets. "We're gonna have a good time," he said. Of course, they always did. Another year, with Mike's cousin Kevan Mueller, they decided to sneak into the pool at John Brown University.

Mike never had a pair of swim trunks that would stay on, and the next time Terry looked, there Mike was, naked as an eel, ready to jump off the high dive. "Our parents never knew half these things!" Terry laughed. "Even so, we got in trouble quite often, but it was worth it."

Once when the boys were helping Don's crew build their new church, Terry recalled the funniest thing that ever happened to them. Out of Don's sight momentarily, Terry and Mike were having water spit fights, each with his own jug of water. A church member dropped by and stared at them suspiciously, eyeing their jugs and watching their foolishness. They imagined what she was thinking, and that made it all the funnier. The joke was too good to halt, so they played it to the finish, laughing so hard they cried.

Terry picked up his jug, took a swig and took off chasing Mike. The woman saw Terry coming and tackled him demanding, "What's in that jug?" He swallowed quickly, not wanting to spit it out at her. "I want to know what's in that jug!" she insisted.

"Water!" he gasped. But she didn't believe him. She grabbed the jug and checked it out for herself before releasing him. Terry is still laughing. Mike and Terry's last time together they ate breakfast at Pannekoeken Huis during Christmas break of '86. Mike excitedly told him about his orders to fly the F-18. "Much of it is computer-flown; but if you make one mistake—it's history," Mike explained.

Terry didn't like the sound of that. "What do you mean, *history*?" he asked. "Well—it's over," Mike answered. "You can't change it. You can't correct it."

Terry's younger brother Tim had disappeared in Sand Creek when they were kids. "He's missing," his pastor told him first. Years later he used the same words to tell Terry about Mike. *It's repeating itself!* Terry thought frantically. "We understand the word, but it's a euphemism, a way to insulate ourselves."

When Mike disappeared, the old, familiar gut-wrenching pain crushed him again. Had he lost another brother? When his minister father later preached that we can go through death triumphantly, inside, the old wall that Terry built when Tim died went up again. "It made me angry to hear him say, 'There is no final end in our existence, and this includes death.' I thought, *Tim is gone, and now Mike, and you say no final end . . . ?*"

Then he felt God's touch through the preaching of the Word. He began to accept in a new way that the Christian life does not end. Terry felt as though God were saying: *Terry, you need to make a transition, a new beginning from the pain and loss you feel. Mike is experiencing new beginnings with Christ. Tim has been experiencing it all these years. Now, it's your turn to begin again.*

This insight didn't ease the pain at first. He had loved his two brothers. What hurt most was not being able to take Mike to breakfast at Pannekoeken Huis to tell him about his new understanding and to see Mike's excitement about God at work in his life.

Both Mike and Tim were blonde. Both got red in the face when they got excited. One day after Tim was gone, Terry substituted for a sixth-grade class. Suddenly, a boy there *was* Tim—identical to his memory of him. It was a painful shock, but he eventually accepted it as good. "Even a picture is good, like the one of Mike and me with that string of bass—never mind the catfish—that we caught that day at the pond."

Terry will always regret he never told Mike that he took the place of his little brother. "I wouldn't have known how to say something like that. But now, I wish he had known . . ." he said.

The next day, Carol and Kirk McIntire arrived with still more of the stories I'd waited to hear. Kirk had only known Mike for two years, but told me about the time he was glad Mike got sick. They had gone deep-sea fishing when a severe storm made Kirk turn green. Feeling like a wimp compared to Mike, the sight of Mike turning green was his only comfort. Kirk thought: *Good. He can spin around in the air in a jet, but he's getting sick deep-sea fishing.*

Vilene Horton had more than one good one to tell on Mike. One exciting night Mike had asked his dad for his truck which was equipped with a CB and an outside loudspeaker, but didn't tell him *why* they wanted it. "Bushwhacking" involved finding a couple making out in a parked car. On that night, Gene Snyman panned the sights with the spotlight while giving a blow by blow account to the world over the CB which also broadcasted through the loudspeaker.

Suddenly, the couple spun around to chase them. Fun at first, Mike drove down Price Road and into a gas station. The couple jumped out and began to throw rocks. Mike stepped on it, more than a little nervous about his dad's truck. He tore out of that predicament into another: flashing lights behind him. A policeman pulled them over. Not knowing what he knew, or what he would say, they waited. "He looked pretty cool and pleased with himself," Vilene recalled. "But all he said was, 'What's your hurry?'"

It sounded innocent enough. Maybe he really didn't know. He made them get out and show their ID's, thinking they had done something—which they had, but not what he thought they had done. Just short of reading their rights, an announcement came over the police radio. They'd caught the ones they were looking for. "Whew! Talk about relief! We weren't as bad as they thought we were!" Vilene laughed.

Finally having heard some orneriness, some foolishness, some little skeletons stashed away, I delighted in it. This hero had taken on the shape and size of a real boy. A massive cloud of witnesses had discovered something in Mike each needs and few receive—unconditional love. It transcended life and death; its strength and power built the foundations of his relationships with businessmen and working women, old people and little children, teenagers and professionals, parents and siblings, mothers and peers.

Mike's mission in life was more than he thought. I couldn't help thinking that even if Mike came back, he still gave his life—his living—for his friends. *There is no greater love than that a man lay down his life for his friends . . .*

But, I'd not yet talked to two pivotal persons from Bartlesville. The strong connecting ligament that bound Mike, Mary Ruth and Gene together seemed wrapped in an opaque sheath, difficult to figure out, impossible to see through. Three lives had developed around one another in significantly unique ways. Each had helped shape the other two into the persons they became. Bound together, they had experienced as one *the wind beneath their wings*. Now remaining behind, the two who waited and searched still felt it lift them.

But those two did not see Mike as a hero. They saw him as someone like themselves—human and flawed. They knew the rest of the story.

CHAPTER 9

THE REST OF THE STORY

O frail and glorious creature, whoever you are,
Cherish this truth: there are hints of glory in your being
seeds of splendor, traces of holiness . . . that's you!
You fragile, noble being, Little-Great-One.
Yes, there are whispers of greatness
in the frail envelope of your being . . .
—Macrina Wiederkehr

Mary Ruth Brown lay on the sofa propped on a pillow. Recovering from surgery, she was captive to my earnest searching for another side to Mike. She had known Mike casually from church and later as English professor for both Mike and Gene. Their relationship deepened during visits to the hospital following Mike's serious eye injury that kept him lying flat for days to prevent hemorrhaging. During that time Mike's buddy, Gene Snyman, was working as an orderly and joined them during his breaks. Sitting on the window ledge, he and Mary Ruth engaged in philosophical discussions. Mike seemed to enjoy it, but didn't participate.

"Dialogue with Mike never seemed to go more than an inch deep," Mary Ruth said. "He bounced around on deep issues, and often based his conclusions on what he had heard and then realized was true rather than personal insights."

When Mike left the hospital, he continued to visit her and always called or took her to lunch when visiting home. "Our extraordinary relationship was very. . . " she hesitated, "ordinary." Not usually attracted to that kind of person, she was amazed at forming an attachment of meaning to Mike. "What was it in me that he needed?" she asked, hardly expecting an answer. Mike was as puzzled by their relationship as she was. Though full of contradictions and tensions, each felt its compelling grasp.

Recognizing herself as an oddity in the conservative Wesleyan Church, Mary Ruth quickly admitted that Mike's attention meant a lot to her because, though conservative himself, he accepted her unconditionally. He was rigid in theory, but not in relationship. "That's what Mike did so well!" she exclaimed.

"If I gave anything to Mike, maybe it was this: With me he could open up and go deeper. I think I touched something in Mike that was missing—a spontaneity of thought, an intuitiveness, a deeper level of thinking, a new way of relating, a new kind of personal quality for him. In our last time together he talked *with me*; we really communicated—not about things, but about us." Representing a daring arena for questioning and exploring, still within safe bounds, Mary Ruth contributed to Mike's success "in the real world" by providing a framework for expanding his world view while still embracing the Christian faith.

Mary Ruth saw Mike as extremely goal-oriented. After he got the F-18 Hornet he said, "I've reached the goal I wanted. What's next?" He thought his God-given charge was to excel at the U.S. Naval Academy, achieve top grades, and finally fly the prestigious F-18 for his country. "But God's gift to the world through Mike was not his discipline, or determination, or goals, but his ability to love and connect with people," Mary Ruth pounced on the purpose of his life. "A light emanated from Mike that illuminated those around him. It didn't illuminate him. It illuminated them. What that spark did, rather than the spark itself, made Mike noteworthy."

Oblivious to his real mission, Mike could not have contrived his God-given capacity to connect with all kinds and all ages of people. It was so much a part of the warp and woof of his personality that everyone knew it was not done for any ulterior motive. Not an act, it was something he had to do, to be, acting from out of the core of his being. That's why people fell all over themselves for Mike.

Mary Ruth shook her head, as though trying to fathom what she called Mike's ability to love—to connect with people. "It was phenomenal," she said. "I merely responded to him. None of it was initiated by me, none at all."

She recounted his numerous acts of kindness that endeared him to her. When he noticed her carpets needed cleaning, he dragged the equipment to her place, worked diligently, then wouldn't accept payment for it. When Mary Ruth spilled nail polish on the carpet, Mike soon arrived to remedy it.

A liberal and a philosopher, Mary Ruth is also amazed that she and Naomi connected in spite of their differences. "I can't escape the deep love I have for her," she revealed. That Naomi was not jealous of her son's relationship with Mary Ruth, she considers a generous and expansive part of Naomi's nature. Kahlil Gibran's words describe Naomi's release of the son she loved:

> Your children are not your children.
> They are the sons and daughters of Life's longing for itself . . .
> You are the bows from which your children as living arrows are sent forth.
> The archer sees the mark upon the path of the infinite, and He bends you with his might that His arrows may go swift and far.
> Let your bending in the Archer's hand be for gladness;

For even as He loves the arrow that flies,
so He loves also the bow that is stable.

Don and Naomi had learned that others give to their children what they cannot, no matter how much they desire to do so. Letting go, both parent and child are liberated. They freed Mike to meet his need for community outside his birth family.

But Mary Ruth understood that even in his great love for people, Mike disdained certain traits or conditions. Pointing to this paradoxical deficit, she said, "To say he lacked compassion sounds strange if you look at all he did for people. Yet, he often did not see the world with empathy, with an expansive heart, with a world view that sees it *as it is*. Instead, he saw the world with judgmental eyes."

Mary Ruth frequently confronted him with his intolerance. Describing their rounds in the ring with animation, she said he threw punches at his sisters, or Lenore, or any woman about her weight, for example. "Getting a little hippy now?" he'd ask, knowing he wouldn't dare say that to her.

Referring to the "righteous fox" list he wrote [Appendix 12], Mary Ruth said, "Young men in their adolescence might do this, but to put down those who don't measure up to the perfect image is a total paradox to his love." Mary Ruth spat out her abhorrence for such emphasis, for such an attack on personhood. "Yet, in spite of himself, God used him as a vehicle of love."

Mike derived great satisfaction out of relationships, but Mary Ruth referred to his insatiable need for attention. "Some people whose need is so great suck it in but can't give it out. Their souls shrivel," she said. "But Mike's intense desire to please God opened the way for God to channel that human need into a capacity to give *and* receive, with both giver and receiver becoming loved and expansive."

Mary Ruth readjusted her pillows. She was opening the rest of the story that most of Mike's friends either did not recognize, or did not talk about. She had questioned him about the realities of war. "Do you ever think of the people that will be blown to pieces, burned and destroyed by the bombs that will fall from your plane?" she asked him.

"No, because I'd be way up there and . . ." Mike shrugged. Mary Ruth flinched. Mike was able to divorce the purpose of the F-18 Hornet from the joy of flying it. Blind to our own errors in human judgment, Mary Ruth and I attempted to untangle the reasons for his oblivion about the purpose of the F-18.

"I think he intuitively knew if he thought about it," Mary Ruth reasoned, "he couldn't do it. Closing that off, he tightened the blinders that interfered with his seeing the world of suffering. Yet, he had this odd proclivity to funnel love—a conundrum." Her brow wrinkled in bewilderment.

"Having said that, I think about how much I miss him." Mary Ruth paused to readjust her position. I paused to reflect. She isn't the kind of person whose ideas go unnoticed. Was she talking about the same man I had met on the streets of Bartlesville? Yet, I'd known Mike's shadow side existed; it does for us all.

"Maybe we ought to allow scientific exploration and learning, fun and expanding horizons, without the cover of military exploitation." Mary Ruth explored the notion that much military technology is developed for the sheer love of it, under the guise of defense and upholding freedom. Without a legitimate purpose for it, the military becomes that "good" cause.

"Fliers and other military personnel cannot find a more intriguing arena to perform for fun, so at times they use military hardware as toys," she argued. "The best and fastest planes are not for fun—they are military. Mike would not have chosen to fly passenger jets, nor was he even out to save the world for American capitalism," she reasoned. "Though intensely patriotic and in love with his country, Mike's real love was for the F-18. His relationship with that plane was one of absolute love. In flying, he was totally fulfilled, at one with God in his Hornet."

I debated. Should I sketch this part of Mike's portrait? Clearly, her perspective on the golden boy dramatically revealed the "whispers of greatness in the frail envelope" of his *being*, as Macrina Wiederkehr wrote. But rather than diminishing who Mike was, this child of God, this child of my heart, assumed even greater proportions. So, I entered the soul of his portrait, viewing the contrasting dark and the light, the textured and the smooth, the obvious and the veiled.

While not excusing the purpose of the machine he loved, Mary Ruth identified with Mike's obsession for flying and the F-18. She understood because she is passionate about her loves. I felt as though we were walking from room to room in our conversation. We entered another with its skylight of hope, asking questions, looking for answers, needing comfort. In our attempt to understand what we were experiencing, we scrutinized what we'd been taught, what we'd learned, and what facing the possibility of Mike's death forced us to question.

Once again I found myself deeply embedded in the unavoidable controversy. Believing neither that pure chance runs rampant nor that God wills everything that happens, Mary Ruth embraces a medieval view that envisions life as a great narrative being written from beginning to end. When an earthly life ends, everything fits into that story. It's not that the author dictates all that happens, but rather that God records the results of human choice and natural laws. When we get to the end and look at what appeared to be tragic accidents and interrupted lives, God, the truly creative writer, will put it all together, resulting in beautiful wholeness. Nothing will be out of place.

In this we all agreed. Naomi would have described the same understanding by quoting from Romans 8:28 [KJV]: " . . . we know that all things work together for good to them that love God . . ."

I interrupted our discussion with a question. "Are you sure you won't write this, Mary Ruth?"

"No," she responded. "But as you write it, remember to look at the scripture narrative. It honestly portrays the whole, demonstrating the glory of a life by showing all sides of it. Look at the great ones—Abraham, David, Moses; Peter and Paul. Examine Mike's whole life—the dark and the light."

Gene would add to the rest of the story. Mary Ruth did not agree with many who considered Mike and Eugene as opposites—Mike as spiritual and Gene as rebel. Instead, she considered their deep spirituality to be the strongest link between them. They grew on each other, needed each other, took from each other. "In fact," Mary Ruth described the connection among the three of them, "it's not what was said, but the interaction among us that is memorable—a symbiotic relationship."

* * * * *

That night, Gene and Kathy arrived at Esther's with their son, Mike's namesake. Finally, we could talk about Mike for the first time since he disappeared.

"I've known Mike since we first visited Bartlesville," Gene began. After Gene's father died, Esther moved the family there. Gene vividly remembered chunks of time with Mike, talking late into the night and noticing Mike's caution about anything questionable, like off-color jokes. Typical boyhood friends, they avoided sensitive or serious issues. Looking back through junior high and high school, Gene had few memories that were not linked with Mike.

Boyhood days were a blur of fun and mischief. Big-scale escapades were usually Gene's ideas with Mike's willing assistance. They brought fireworks to basketball games and to camp—outlawed, of course. They rigged one contraption that could fire a pop-bottle rocket every five minutes, while the inventors innocently and conspicuously hung out with the adults.

Gene often teased Mike about taking notes on sermons or memorizing scriptures incessantly. One day the two decided that a room in the church tower ought to be a youth room. With permission, they started sawing, hammering, piecing together, hardly within building codes. When Don saw their determination, his construction crew finished it. Mike and Gene initiated it by taking their BB guns to the tower. "We let 'em have it," he laughed, "and watched the unsuspecting people dance down below!"

Gene remembered fondly that Mike had a certain embarrassed sweetness about him that caused him to punch on Gene whenever he'd get nervous. And Mike could cry. After holding the emotional reins tightly for years after his father's death, Gene, too, began making the connection between events and feelings. He became more vulnerable, more human—more like Mike.

Mike was patient and pedantic when teaching Gene, though he cringed when he heard the grinding gears of his meticulously pampered motorcycle. At the same time, Gene possessed street savvy that Mike lacked. Mike often went to him, believing he'd know the answers and not make fun of him publicly.

Once while planning a camping trip, one boy suggested that including girls might complicate things. "What if one of them gets her period?" someone asked. Mike blurted out, "Period? What's that?" Embarrassed, their only response was, "Good grief, Mike." He later nabbed Gene, "Okay Gene, what are they talking about?"

Adamant about the Christian way of life, Mike maintained strict standards for himself, and even for those he didn't know, while at the same time giving his friends unconditional acceptance. Mary Ruth had confronted Mike on the inconsistency of allowing his deep love for Gene to extend the boundaries for him in ways he wouldn't for others. Gene assented with this story.

While stationed for three years at the Pentagon in the

Army while Mike attended the Naval Academy, Gene one year planned a St. Patrick's Day party. Then, Mike asked about visiting for the weekend. As Mike didn't accept that Christians can drink alcoholic beverages, Gene warned him he would serve beer. "Furthermore," Gene leveled with Mike, "I'll drink too." Mike reacted with a momentary look of desperate anxiety, but responded, "No problem." Gene knew Mike still accepted him.

In adulthood, their differences became even more pronounced. For awhile, Gene no longer saw any future in his relationship with Mike. They were too far apart. Impervious to any denial of their friendship, Mike continued to write, leaving Gene feeling bad because he wasn't intentional about nurturing it. "I'm in touch with a God who is more than the Bible, or the church. It's a bigger God I have," Gene defended himself. Of course, Mike, too, stressed he was in touch with a "bigger God" who is more than the Bible or the church, albeit through a personal relationship with Jesus Christ.

While Gene was opening his feelings, Mike was opening his mind. "Mike is closed-minded in some ways," Gene continued. "Yet, he understands. He sees something in me—in people like me—that he wants." Gene, slipping into present tense every so often, talked as though Mike were sitting in the same room, listening to our attempts to figure him out.

In one class at the Academy Mike studied Tolstoy and C.S. Lewis. Discussing the readings with him, Gene saw in Mike a hunger to know God in an even deeper and more authentic way. In their conversations about what seemed to be secular, Mike began to recognize that even there, God is present.

"To continue his search demanded courage that challenged even the exemplary Marine," Gene said. "He had so much invested in his prescribed picture of God, and it was so fundamental to him, that to deny it would be to deny his whole person. But the reason Mike had a future—and that we finally had a future together—was that he became teachable,"

Gene concluded. In his intense desire to live for God, Mike finally allowed himself to wonder and articulate questions, however cautiously, with two of his friends: Mary Ruth and Gene.

Contrasting his own lack of discipline with Mike's strong commitment to self-discipline and spiritual regimens, Gene nonetheless had a strong sense that something, or someone in him, was teaching him. He relates it to the *Voice* that Plato understood. Yet watching Mike, Gene saw that discipline is not only necessary, but good.

"Without a dad, and having a mom who catered to me, I grew up differently than Mike. I needed the influence of discipline, while Mike needed to explore the deeper meanings of life and death," he said.

Together, yet separately, each had developed a broader, more holistic understanding of God, relationships and themselves. Gene, too, recognized the symbiosis that Mary Ruth had emphasized as the mystery that bound the three together. The three friends completed, or fulfilled one another, giving and receiving what each needed. That triumvirate provided space to explore rather than to conform. Each attempted to affirm what was *unlike the other*, expressions of God's image in each person. Giving themselves in that uniqueness to one another, the three became more nearly whole in a relationship that strengthened them as individuals.

As an adult, Gene began to understand friendship in a new way. He recognized a piety in what they had, which he now recognizes in all relationships. "An emotional piece of me belongs forever to that person. Old girlfriends—thank goodness, Kathy understands that—or anyone I once loved cannot be totally dismissed or forgotten. Part of that person will always be there," Gene realized. "I owe that to Mike. I owe our history that."

Then Gene became exuberant, speaking in the present tense again. "There is a certain sensitivity and understanding growing in Mike!" Flying the F-18 seemed part of the breakthrough for him, as though in crashing through the barriers of gravity and sound, new sensations and understanding invaded him.

"Imagine! Mike began to write *poetry*." Gene shook his head incredulously. "If Mike hadn't kept in touch, I would have lost so much more than one friend. I owe a debt to Mike for those people who are now my friends because Mike connected with me so deeply. He paved the way to meaningful friendship."

A few months before Mike disappeared, Gene and Mike spent an evening together. They talked the night away in Gene's 4-wheel-drive Toyota. Like Mary Ruth, when Gene left Mike, he knew something was changing. "Our friendship has a future!" Gene was ecstatic, definitely living in the present again. He sensed Mike's growth, his breaking away from the last vestiges of what bound him, his openness to new thinking. Both placed a premium on their future, on the new path they were exploring together.

Mike had given a Lladro sculpture to Gene and Kathy. "Whatever rolls your socks down," he had said, grinning. Purely unselfish and thoughtful, it was not something Mike would ever want himself, and it touched Gene deeply. He began to consider the kind of gift he could give Mike to symbolize their growth and friendship. It would have to be something of beauty. Hard. Hurting. Healing. One-of-a-kind. Expensive. Hand-hewn. In time, it came to him: a hunting knife, created by an artisan.

There would be three of them. At last the first one was ready—for Mike. The second knife was already commissioned for another buddy, Ken Hada. The third would be Gene's. The casing sheaths would be hand-tooled leather. He could hardly wait to give it to Mike, to show him he understood, to represent them together, to embody both their past and their future. Gene often envisioned the way it would be when Mike opened it. He'd go crazy over it. He decided to wait for that moment until they got together for the wedding . . .

Mary Ruth was the first to tell Gene about Mike's plane disappearing. Feeling the strength of their triune bond, it was as though the three were still together. When Gene heard the news, he talked aloud to Mike. And Mike listened. Gene didn't try to analyze what was happening, and he didn't recall what he said, but that moment in Mike's presence was real to Gene, like a reverent prayer. "I know Mike heard me," Gene said simply.

Gene recalled an earlier incident when Mike nearly disappeared from his life. Hunting with Mike, Gene was carrying his loaded gun over his shoulder when he accidentally pulled the trigger. The bullet whizzed over Mike. They sat down weakly to recover from the fright. Gene revealed to Mike his fear of losing someone he loved, even as he had lost his father.

"When Mike disappeared," Gene said, "I agonized over who should receive the hunting knife." Certainly, Mary Ruth had no need for it. Maybe Don? It wouldn't mean much to him; Mike had never touched it. If he gave it to Lenore, it might go to a husband some day; it would mean nothing to him. Finally, Gene put it away, a gift without a recipient. He sometimes draws it from the sheath and rubs his hand over the shining steel coldness of the glimmering blade. At times he carries it with him—a symbol, a piece of Mike and Gene together.

I pulled out some pictures of Mike he hadn't seen. Quietly staring, he said, "When I look at pictures like this, it's as if I am *there* for a moment. Then the pain comes, the pain of nostalgia that follows the joy of nostalgia. As I look, I can almost touch something tangible—it's right there, within reach. Then suddenly I realize, he is not really there. That's why a person stares and stares at a picture, trying to recapture the person, the instant, the feeling again."

I joined him there for a moment. We silently looked at Mike. We lived the joy and the pain together again.

Gene and Mary Ruth had led me more deeply into Mike.

I had heard the rest of the story. I had seen glimpses of Mike that many of his friends had missed or been unable to articulate. Mike was still missing. Marilyn Ginsberg was still investigating her husband's disappearance. The parents were still praying. Lenore was still waiting. And some were still searching.

In my own search, it was time to follow Mike's journey as a U.S. Marine aviator. I would begin at the Naval Academy. Where would it lead?

CHAPTER 10

THE MAKING OF AN AVIATOR

He parted the heavens and came down;
dark clouds were under his feet.
He climbed the cherubim and flew;
he soared on the wings of the wind.
—Psalm 18:9-11

United States Naval Academy:
Summer 1980 to Spring 1984

Ginny Krenning and her family "adopt" scores of young people who enter the USNA as Plebes and leave as officers. She and her family spend hours watching their "sons" in parades, cheering Navy football games and praying during their jumps into the cornfield as they earn their wings.

Before Mike's first drill as Company Commander, his buddies had devised a way to fasten his sword in the sheath. When the big moment arrived, Mike grasped the sword to draw it out with the prescribed flourish. It was hopelessly attached. Watching, Mike's adopted family and roommate howled with laughter.

Majoring in oceanography and meteorology, academics challenged him. He sometimes wrote, "I have a whole minute before I must run to the next thing on my list!" He relished every sport he added to those he already loved, including sailing 500 miles from the Academy to the Bahamas. But he raved most about parachuting, receiving his silver wings as a junior and gold wings as a senior. Next came skydiving. He wrote his parents, "I want to free fall, starting at 10,000 feet. The best part is that it's so cheap. I'll let you know what I decide, but start praying. Think how good I am for your prayer life—I really keep you on your toes!"

Mick Rovenstine knew Mike as an older buddy from home who preceded him to the Academy. Typical of the clueless Plebe, Mick usually had no idea what was going on. On one occasion Mick set off to visit Mike's room on the other side of Bancroft Hall where seniors live. Aware of his lowly status, he passed gingerly by the intimidating upperclassmen.

Plebes are required to greet all upperclassmen appropriately, as: "Good evening, Sir," with the accent on *sir* to distinguish it from greetings for ordinary human beings. Unfortunately, assuming one young fellow who passed him was a custodian, Mick failed to address him. But it just so happened he was *not* a custodian. He chewed Mick up and spat him out with disdain and arrogance for his failure to greet him respectfully. Also unfortunately, the incident happened just outside Mike's door where he laughed uproariously inside.

Now a Marine pilot himself, Mick often asks in tough situations, "What would Mike do?"

As part of the curriculum at USNA, Mike served on the USS Midway in the South Pacific. Reports of his performance there included such notations as these.

> Grades of A (4.0) in every category: working relations, professional knowledge, attitude/motivation, application/industry, ability to speak in an effective manner, seamanship, watchstanding, judgment, personal behavior, military bearing, maturity, imagination, forcefulness, analytical ability, reliability, and growth potential.

> Midshipman Mueller has excelled in all areas . . . self starter, enthusiastic learner, uncanny ability to identify problems and propose solutions before the problems occur, intelligent and energetic individual with exceptionally keen insight regarding personnel problems. A recognized leader, frequently sought out for advice, both on and off the flight deck . . . accomplished more in his four week cruise than most officers do in their first year . . . experienced the "black shoe" side of the Navy . . . motivated . . . a credit to the Naval Academy . . . will make an excellent officer and strong leader . . . bright wit, pleasant personality . . .

Mike's ability to combine genuine friendliness with professional excellence, courtesy and dignity, provided the privilege of an assignment as escort for Prince Albert of Monaco, son of Princess Grace (Kelly), when he visited the States.

Carlos Kizzie, Mike's roommate for three years, had disappeared from my search as surely as Mike. A law school student at Georgetown University, at last he called. We drove to the Academy in Annapolis, Maryland. His first memories of Mike were of a sandy-haired, well-liked kid with a midwestern drawl.

"Just as life starts with some rubber-gloved doctor hitting you when you haven't done anything to deserve it, USNA starts with plebe summer," Carlos described it succinctly. As roommates they enjoyed each other, got sick of each other, fell down and picked each other up, and shared their deepest desires. Mike liked things neat and was out of sorts until they were. "An irritating roommate, he was the Felix Unger, and I was the Oscar Madison," Carlos laughed. "He was perfect for me, setting a standard of orderliness and excellence." Mike kidded that they were stuck together like "ugly to an ape."

They attended church regularly with Steinberg and Hollingsworth and even sneaked in early morning meetings in the "head" (restroom) for fellowship. But fear of being caught severely handicapped their praying. Mike quickly distinguished himself in self-discipline and modeled the ability to focus on a task. Mike's personality and lifestyle became the candle and Carlos the flame that attracted classmates to their room. While Carlos could quickly acquaint himself with a hundred classmates, Mike developed a friendship like he would scrub a sink—carefully and meticulously. Carlos saw Mike as a man of depth in thought and emotion. Never having had such a close relationship with anyone, Carlos said that experience paved the way for communication in his marriage.

After graduation, sporadic letters kept Carlos and Mike aware of their location, but they didn't worry about each other. That a plane would land on Carlos's office on the Yuma flight line was more likely than Mike's disappearance in a jet. Shortly before he disappeared, Mike flew a training hop into Yuma. Carlos recalled it was Mike's love of flying that kept him from going to a military doctor when he sprained his ankle while running with Carlos there. "No military doctor will ground me," Mike laughed.

Then, the world suddenly stopped spinning. Carlos ran into an old classmate one day who told him a plane from Mike's squadron had just disappeared. Knowing that he and Mike were roommates at the Academy, he didn't mention Mike was missing, even though he knew. "What would I have done in the middle of Camp Pendleton Base Exchange had I discovered my first true friend might have died?"

Clutching the phone, scarcely able to force the words from his desert-dry lips, Carlos dialed Mike's squadron. Identifying himself as Mike's Academy roommate, he told the XO what he'd heard. "In that split-second hesitation, I knew," Carlos said. His clerk knew too, by the look on Carlos's face. The Yuma base was an 850 Marine/sailor squadron, but that day Carlos left it all in the hands of the Lance Corporal as he stumbled helplessly along the flight line and taxiways for hours.

"I rarely cry," Carlos said, "but that day in uniform, watching Marine helicopters and jets take off, I cried. I hated Mike for doing that to me. I hated the other fool pilots for doing what they do and for loving it. I hated the other pilots for coming back when Mike didn't. Most of all, I hated me for not telling Mike when I had the chance just how much he meant to me."

Carlos wanted to stay in touch with Mike's family, but, instead, for years he avoided the pain of those precious memories and relationships with the Muellers. At last he was ready to crack the protective shell.

Quantico and Naval Air Test Center, Patuxent, Maryland Summer 1984 to Spring 1985

In August of 1984, Mike joined our family in Springfield to become a "real" son with his own room and an open door for nearly a year. After receiving his commission in the U.S. Marine Corps and appointment to aviation training, his initial assignment was The Basic School (TBS) in Quantico, Virginia. The gruelling weeks that stretched from late summer into the cold of winter sent him scurrying up the Interstate 95 corridor to our home on his free days.

Mike enhanced the image of the tough Marine with stories of the battles and the jumps, the pain and the studies that shaped him into 2 LT Michael D. Mueller, USMC. One bitterly cold day, I drove to Quantico to see the completion ceremonies. With the Krenning family, I watched, thankful and proud as any parent, as Mike marched onto the field.

While waiting for placement in flight school, Mike was first stashed at the Naval Air Systems Command in Washington, D.C., and during the last three months at the Patuxent (PAX) Naval Air Test Center in Maryland. He frequently flew helos and turbo props, accumulating 75 flight hours. "What an awesome three months!" he laughed. "It almost made up for six months of misery in Quantico."

Finally, after Mike disappeared, I would visit PAX.

Following a couple hours on the road and lunch at The Roost, a local restaurant that had become a shrine for all who had passed through on their way to becoming pilots and astronauts, I followed Major Waggaman into a cavernous hangar. Men and women there service the giant jets amidst the noise that hit me like a blast of cold air. Donning a helmet, I climbed onto a scaffold that put me eye-to-eye with an F-18.

Had such a favored retreat, such a valued place of worship, such a cockpit home Mike loved so much, also become his tomb? Behind me, peering into the cockpit, the major bellowed that the Hughes APG-655 radar screen provides day and night long-range detection and tracking of airborne targets, adverse weather, and unique raid assessment modes to identify closely-spaced targets.

Shouting above the roar of motors and machinery, the major dropped information like little bombs that informed my understanding but bombarded my sensitivity. Pointing to the Head-Up Display (HUD), the primary flight instrument, he shouted, "It serves as the weapons delivery control center." I wanted to forget that's what this love affair of Mike's included.

Standing under its belly, MAJ Waggaman continued: " . . . machine gun shoots 6 thousand 20mm bullets per minute . . ." More shouting. More explanations. More information than I could later remember. I'd seen enough. Driving away from PAX, I stopped by the river to clear my brain, to sort out my feelings. So that's what Mike couldn't wait to navigate: The F/A-18 Hornet, the fighter/attack jet I'd just explored.

Pensacola and Whiting Field, Florida:
Summer 1985 to Spring 1986

Having been offered a place to write in Florida, where I would also finally meet Mike's Academy friend Lance, I gratefully accepted. He had invited me to stay with him overnight. When he opened the door of his apartment, I gasped. He looked like Mike. The same welcoming eyes and a perennial tan. Same height and sun-streaked light, short-cropped hair. Same crinkles around his eyes and clean-shaven, freshly-scrubbed face. Same kind of casual shorts and t-shirt.

"You must be Lance—you look like Mike!" I laughed.

"Guess we're the cookie-cutter image," he smiled broadly. Within five minutes we were lost in Mike. We drove over to Whiting Field where Lance was an instructor pilot. He outlined the progression of a Marine from the Academy to Navy aviator. Following their commission at the Academy, Marines go to The Basic School; all Navy and Marine pilots begin flight training in Pensacola with Aviation Indoctrination (AI) that includes academic and physical conditioning, followed by primary flight training for 22 weeks at Whiting Field.

"At that point," Lance continued, "they apply for one of three routes: jets, helos, props." He waved with a smile to the security officer and parked with no questions asked. I glanced at his youthful profile again. "It's more than looking like Mike," I began. "Seeing you, it's as if I'm with him again." Lance was quiet. "Thanks a lot," he said simply.

We strolled toward the field. The single-prop T-34 C's looked like toy planes, all glinting orange-winged and orange-nosed. "That's what they all fly first," Lance explained. "They're painted orange to tell everyone up there to avoid them." I laughed to picture Mike so humiliated, then remembered his essay for family and friends about completing his first solo in one of those things—he didn't sound humiliated at all [See Appendix 10].

Lance offered to let me climb up to look inside one of those loved and pampered T-34 C's. Young pilots were everywhere: underneath, beside, inside, on top of them, just as Mike had done, learning, thinking, studying, dreaming big. Several flew overhead under the billowing cumulus clouds. The day was perfect. Always exciting, always different, always unpredictable.

Like Mike, Lance loved it. "I'd rather fly than anything,"

he said. "Everything works towards getting up there the next time." I've never met a military pilot who felt differently. They're happiest when flying—or, talking flying. Lance tried to explain their obsession. "For some, flying is like a religious experience; for others, it's the God-like control of machinery worth millions; for some it's like sex; for still others it's the sheer ecstasy of breaking natural law when gravity is stripped of power. Earth, people, problems—they stay on earth."

Then I asked again the ultimate question we all sought to understand. "How might Mike have crashed, Lance? What *pilot error* might it have been?" "That's the tricky thing about flying," he answered thoughtfully. "A pilot is trained to always think: *What's next? What do I do next?* If the pre-flight is done right, the paraloft (parachute) will open. If there's a flame-out, he's trained in the next step. He builds on each successive moment, continually assessing data. It plays itself out in concrete, concise, controlled action. But, pilots are human," he shrugged.

"A Navy career pilot has about a 25 percent chance of dying an accidental death. You're continually making decisions, and when you're going five miles a minute or faster, the quickest decisions may not be quick enough and . . . " his voice trailed off. For some reason the conversation was unnerving. It sounded as though Lance didn't doubt that Mike may have crashed for any number of reasons, and that *pilot error* means *any* reason.

That evening we watched and listened as Mike joined us on the video taken of their fun in the swimming pool four days before Mike disappeared. They had attended church together and planned to meet—with Lenore—in Hawaii soon. Mike was real, vibrant, alive as we heard his laugh and watched him swim on the tape. When we recovered our voices and capped our emotions, we began to talk about the purpose beneath this passion for flying fighter aircraft that pervades the elite, the elect of this profession.

I told Lance that when I visited PAX Naval Air Station and climbed the scaffold to get a good look at the controls of the F-18, the pilot there exuded the usual excitement about his machine. It was infectious. I felt the unmitigated joy that Mike often tried to communicate—until we went beneath its belly to examine the purpose for the plane. I explained to Lance that while the major explained the sequence for releasing the ordnance, his voice had seemed to drift farther and farther away. Even as his voice shouted on above the din, the sound seemed to recede. I had silently asked Mike, hoping he was listening, *How could you, Mike? How could you ever have done this to human beings?*

Lance nodded sympathetically. Here was a pilot who really seemed to hear me. "I think that Mike would say this: *I'd rather be in the position to do this than have someone up there who can't be trusted to use good judgment,"* Lance said. "Mike always would rather do something himself to be sure it was done right."

I recalled the excitement Mike expressed in his letters during this phase: "I can't wait to drop bombs and shoot 20 mm guns! I just got back from Yuma, Arizona, where we practiced dropping bombs. Of course, no one uses this antiquated method anymore, but we have to get the basics. It's a lot of fun, but I really don't relish *dropping bombs on anyone* . . . "

That's what I thought Mike was going to say. That's what I wanted to believe he would say. But what he really said was: *It's a lot of fun, but I really don't relish the idea of someone shooting back.*

Lance shrugged and leaned forward, his elbows on his knees. He sat in deep thought without answering. Then he reached for the JAG manual and the MIR, and settled down to examine the three-inch thick black notebook of reports, questions, letters—all collected by Mike's parents since May 20, 1987. Flipping pages, he compared one page with another, looking for clues, searching for reasons, seeking consolation—or hope.

"So, what makes a pilot an *aviator*, Lance?" I interrupted. Time was running out. I'd be on my way in the morning and still needed to learn more. "Makes . . . a pilot . . . an aviator . . ." Lance repeated tentatively, thinking aloud. "Pilots are born, not made," he said.

It's hard to explain to anyone outside that fraternity of young fighter jocks. To begin with, one in three who choose to fly never make it off the ground. After they get into the program, one by one the incompetent slide from their tenuous hold on the ladder to the top. Equalled by none, the few that make it can talk of little else. Flying is their first love.

"Mike had that self-confidence, that independence, that big ego that made that possible," Lance looked at me sideways, almost apologetically, as if suggesting that Mike had a big ego might taint my image of him. I only laughed. Tom Wolfe had written in *The Right Stuff*: "The Pilot Ego—it doesn't come any bigger!"

The goal for these aviators is all-encompassing. It's as if family, friends, the past, the future, and anyone outside the "brotherhood" become minuscule dots on a landscape far below their flying life. Perhaps that is one reason for the slow acceptance of women aviators, legislating against sexism, penalizing such behavior as in the Tailhook incident . . . on and on.

Yet, something about Mike didn't exactly fit the image of the aviator personality. We tried to pinpoint it. "Unlike many of the young fighter jocks, he, uh . . . he was able to take the same, sometimes obnoxious, qualities typical of fighter pilots and make them work," Lance said. He had encapsulated a truth about Mike. Mike could translate his self-confidence into God-confidence: *I can do all things* rings with arrogance. But he shifted the emphasis toward a profound confidence in God as his strength: "I can do all things through him who gives me strength" (Philippians 4:13).

Added to that was Mike's relationship with people that also registered a full ten in priorities. His letters to male buddies, old girlfriends, women, children, couples, moms, boyhood chums, former teachers and pastors, relatives, professors, secretaries, teenagers—even his insurance agent—would fill a museum. He said *I love you*, and meant it, in a hundred different ways to as many different people.

"But that's not to say everyone loved Mike," Lance backed off. "Some guys did *not* appreciate Mike's ideals and convictions. Once, when Mike was Company Commander and I was battalion leader, we flew to California for a Navy game. Some of the guys took liquor on the flight—positively forbidden. Mike found out about it and—true to form—reported the offenders. No, not everyone loved Mike," Lance chuckled.

"On the other hand," Lance remembered, "some guys at the Academy were positively obnoxious about their beliefs, from religion to the Redskins. I never saw Mike try to jam his convictions down anyone's throat."

Navy aviators know there is no such thing as *final cuts*—they must continually *make it*. Even an eye exam can catapult the flyer into a desk job or an ATC room. They never forget that *incompetence* can mean merely that the eyesight suddenly slides toward myopia. You can't spend 24 hours with a Navy pilot without the subject of eyesight surfacing. Mike spoke of passing a routine eye exam with reverence and awe, as though spared the angel of death one more time. Perhaps it's the only time these aviators feel humility. Even Lance mentioned in our first hours together that he was thankful his eyesight is perfect: "It's 20/20. It can't waver," he said. "That's a primary measuring tool."

If arches fall, or blood pressure escalates, or Charlie horses grab the calves, the young jock is done for, finished. Though not considered failures by those outside the fraternity, nonetheless, a silent recognition and fear momentarily attaches its tentacles around others in the squadron. To have come so far, and then to lose *it*—that tenuous elevated position far above other earthlings—crushes the spirit. Yes, you either had *it*, or you didn't.

Ranked as equal in importance with the physiological component are emotional stability and academic performance. Mike finished in the top 5 percent of his class of 900. "But, I wouldn't call Mike brilliant," Lance said. "He studied all the time." He was right. I pictured Mike sitting on our patio in Virginia amid leftover snapdragons and fall mums, studying diligently even on the weekends.

The pilots who make helos or props continue at Whiting Field. If they get jets, they go to Kingsville or Beeville, Texas, or Meridian, Mississippi. Then finally, they're ready to select the aircraft they hope to fly permanently. Mike had top grades and he picked the latest and the greatest—the F-18.

Indeed, Mike had all *the right stuff*—plus. Maybe. Unless Tom Wolfe's designation includes only those pilots who ultimately make it to retirement without an aircraft mishap.

Lance had painted the journey of an aviator, adding vivid detail to the splashes of color in the stories of Mike's friends and family. The rhythm of life, as predictable yet changing as the nearby Gulf of Mexico, confounded us. Into the night we considered the ebb and flow of possibilities, of unanswered questions, of our understanding of God in all these memories.

The next morning I hugged Lance goodbye outside the Waffle House where we'd lingered over coffee. Promising to keep in touch, he called a few days later. Subdued, he told me he'd been especially busy. One of the IP's had gone down with a student in one of those little orange T-34 C's that I'd checked out a few days earlier.

Not Lance, thank God, I thought. Feeling suddenly guilty for my selfish thoughts, I prayed for the wives and children, parents and friends left to mourn two more Navy pilots. I could hardly bear to hear Lance's pain, or to associate what I'd experienced with Mike with yet more grieving families. I hung up in a fresh torrent of tears. This was more than a story.

It was everyday reality. If not for me, it was for someone else.

What a way to live, always vulnerable, yet loving it so much they can't give it up until it gives them up.

Chase Field in Beeville, Texas:
Spring 1986 to Spring 1987

It was this phase of training that included the T-2 Buckeye trainer jet, learning to land on a carrier at sea, getting his gold wings, and finally choosing the kind of jet in which he planned to dedicate his flying career. Mike qualified in the T-2 Buckeye on May 22, 1986—just short of one year from the date he would disappear.

No sooner had I decided I needed to experience a carrier take-off and landing myself, than I resolved to forego that encounter after reading an engaging clip from the *Pensacola News Journal* on Monday, April 18, 1988. Written by Elizabeth Donovan, the headline read: *Disaster Looms Every Workday.*

> . . . You've got lap and chest straps—four to be exact. Then there's a helmet complete with padded goggles. Goggles? Padded? Isn't anybody optimistic? Finally, there's what I call the "death mode" position in preparation for the catapult shot: Chin on chest, arms crossed, hands clutching straps, shins pressed to the seat ahead. We wait for almost an hour before launching—me biting my lip like it was my last meal. Then we get the signal to assume the death mode position. I hope the pilot's having a good day. The Navy does this all the time; pilots do it every day. Yeah, but not with me on board.
>
> Who invented this anyway? Did his mother know about it? Hooooooooooooly cooooooooooooow. Zero to 117 knots in three seconds. Face mashed, goggles skewed, shins carved. But we're off! By George, it worked . . .

Mike practiced his own landings on the USS Lexington during the Beeville phase of jet training. After 48 years of service for 50,000 pilots, including Mike, the Lex was retired on November 7, 1991. Following qualification for carrier landings on January 25, 1987, Mike wrote about it from the pilot's perspective [See Appendix 11].

Next, Mike's winging on March 6, 1987, changed everything. The occasion evoked joy and laughter, respect and honor from family, friends, and those who promoted him to that golden moment. Lenore, Don and Naomi, the Ekstroms, his roommate Bill Jeffries, and a host of friends from the First Baptist Church he attended joined in the day-long celebration.

"Not only did Mike stand out head and shoulders above the others who received their wings that day, he walked taller, sat straighter than all the rest," Edna Ekstrom bragged. After a last flight in the T-2 before receiving his wings, Mike walked toward his peers in the squadron who met him with the ritual of ice-dousing. After stripping off his g-suit and boots, he was led to a chair. They then drenched the back of his neck into his shirt and pants with buckets-full of ice water while Naomi and the other women screamed. At last they allowed him to stand up. Shaking out the ice cubes, he received the "wet-boot award." He had passed the last—and easiest— hurdle.

During the formal ceremony that afternoon, the Commanding Officer reminded the audience that the first U.S. astronaut, the first U.S. astronaut to orbit the earth, and the first human being on the moon were each Navy aviators, and that similar opportunities awaited these graduates.

He described the planes that can jam enemy aircraft and escort planes into enemy territory. "We entrust these planes to these young aviators sitting here," the CO paused dramatically. I'm not sure what the eight new aviators felt, but a look of awe and a quiver of excitement registered on the faces of those who observed their sons and brothers, husbands and friends.

"You can be proud of them," he told the audience. "They

survived the physical, mental, and academic cuts. Of course, they are already very cocky," he smiled, "but there are good reasons for that. It is in this phase that they practice being a *killer pilot* rather than just an aircraft pilot."

There it was again, the F-18 pilot is a killer. I didn't like to think about it. The euphemisms, the patriotism, the glorification, "all pomp and circumstance of war" sounds so good, if you just don't think. The CO observed that beyond the heroes lost, it does us good to look at the larger group represented by them. Then he read these words by columnist George Will, written after the Challenger tragedy.

> Right now, somewhere around the world, young men are landing high performance jet aircraft on pitching decks of aircraft carriers—at night. You can't pay people to do that. They do it out of love of country, of adventure, of the challenge. We all benefit from it, and the very fact that we don't have to think about it tells us how superbly they are doing their job. Living on the edge of danger so the rest of us need not think about, let alone experience danger . . .

"That's these gents right here," the CO pointed to the eight. Then Bill Jeffries presented the candidates to receive their gold wings. Bill added a personal farewell to Mike: "Mike is my roommate. I'll *really* miss him . . ." He hesitated. I blinked back tears, then laughed when he continued, "because he's taking the microwave!"

NAS Lemoore:
April to May 20, 1987

The information I still needed from Lemoore NAS goaded me on in my search. The map of Mike's journey from the United States Naval Academy to the F/A-18 at Lemoore NAS was nearly complete. But before leaving for California, I'd talk to someone else who loved to fly: Mike's soul brother Alan Chamberlain. Unlike Carlos and Lance who hid behind their pain for their missing brother, my nephew maintained his balance by talking. I drove to Denton, Texas, where I would hear Alan's story.

He closed the door behind us and began.

◀ Mike with his sister Nadean.

▲ Mike showed his love of planes from boyhood, here posing at an air show.

▼ Mike as best man at Gene Snyman's wedding.

▲ Mike and his roommate, Carlos Kizzee, strut their "stuff" at the U.S. Naval Academy.

▲ Mike on assignment as the escort to Prince Albert of Monaco.

▲ Mueller family portrait in 1985.

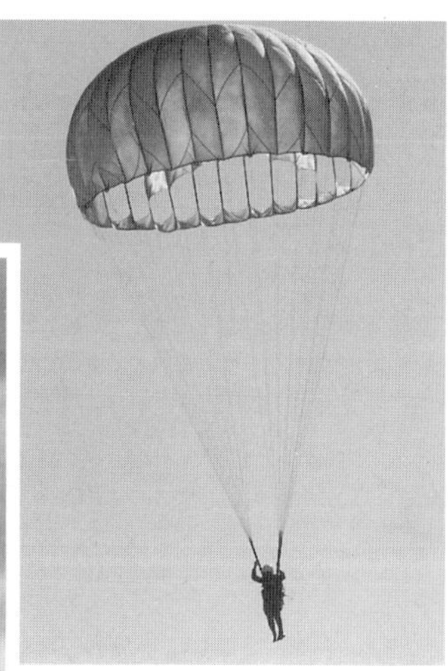

▲ Mike parachuted at every opportunity.
◀ Mike wears his newest set of "wings."

▲ Mike and Alan Chamberlain on their motorcyle trip.

◀ Engagement picture of Mike and Lenore.

▼ They celebrate at a party after Mike's "winging."

▼▶ Mike hanging out with the machines he loved to fly.

◀ Mike's grave in Arlington National Cemetery.

▼ Kavanaugh Ridge, site of Mike's plane crash.

CHAPTER 11

FLYING ON WEDNESDAY

. . . David bowed down before Jonathan three times
with his face to the ground. Then they kissed each other
and wept together—but David wept the most.
Jonathan said to David, "Go in peace,
for we have sworn friendship with each other
in the name of the Lord . . ."
—I Samuel 20:41-42

Their first adventure together included Mike's cousin Kevan when Alan was about six. Mike was too young to ride a bike, so he climbed on the back of Alan's. They started down a hill that dead-ended, and Kevan sped off to the right to go home. Alan yelled to Mike, "Right or left?" No response. Picking up speed, Alan yelled louder, "*Right or left*?" And still he didn't answer. "Being the idiot I was at the time," Alan laughed, "when we reached the bottom of the hill, I couldn't make up my mind, so I just went straight." Both flew off the bike and ended up in what felt like a cactus garden. In a pile of debris with the bike and both boys tangled together, Alan groaned out, "Mike, why didn't you say something? Why not just give me a right or left answer?"

"Well," Mike said, "I was pointing. I don't know my right

or left." Now, when Alan pictures him flying a 25 million-dollar jet, he laughs to remember it.

"The effects of this thing were immediate," Alan said in his slow Texas drawl that sort of dribbles over you like blackstrap molasses until you are glued to every word, no matter how long it takes. Alan had never lost anyone close to him. Having his friend disappear for what had been a year by that time, brought him up short. Listening to him made me feel I was eavesdropping in a confessional, but Alan wanted to talk about his new commitment to God.

"I loved Mike so much," Alan went on. "Sometimes I think God let us renew our friendship so this event would straighten me out. This is kinda personal, but I've increased my time spent with God, just sitting quietly in God's presence, letting God talk with me. I'm in a Bible study group and active in my church. I can't tell anyone adequately how much Mike has shaped my life and how God is changing me. Many things have done a 180 degree turn."

"It's not so much what happens to us, but our reactions to life that are important," Alan concluded. "Maybe God wants us to see things in a new way. If Mike's gone, am I going to let it affect the way I live? Is it just going into my memory, but not changing the way I *feel* about things? Will I encourage anybody to live the higher life?"

Watching God supply the needs of Don and Naomi through the tragedy of confused waiting, Alan believes God is at work for him also. In his roofing business, he's amazed at his boldness in witnessing about his new relationship with God as he tells people about Mike.

Meditating on the unpredictability of life, Alan immersed himself in planning a high school band reunion to honor their old, retired band director. "What good would it do to eulogize him when he dies? That celebration made him so happy," he said. "He got to be with old friends. The people closest to him expressed what they felt. We didn't wait for the box." Emphasizing his new priorities Alan said, "It's affected every relationship. I now tell someone when I love them—even my little sister."

"Most Christians I've known are older adults, kinda beyond my interests and not experiencing the same kinds of temptations that face me. But Mike *did* grow up in the same world I did. He understood what it was like for a single guy to live in the world. In putting God first, he was a *tremendous encouragement* to me."

The impact of Mike's memorial service in Bartlesville gave birth to a startling realization of the cost of freedom. Just prior to the Gulf War Alan said, "My generation hasn't seen the wars. Friends just ten years older know what it's like to see your brother come home in a box. If Mike is really gone—I ask myself whether I'm willing to pay that price."

Alan also searched for answers by exploring how God's will permits tragedy. As he looked at the scriptures and at history, he glimpsed Isaiah sawn in half. Paul beheaded. Peter crucified upside down. "I wouldn't have picked that for any of those guys," he said. "And for Mike? I'd never have picked this for him."

"I once asked Mike: *Bud, what are you going to do in case of war? Doesn't that concern you, being sent out on a mission and maybe not coming back?* Mike just kinda shrugged," Alan said.

"Oh yea, I've thought about it," Mike answered. "I figure if it happens, it happens. It seems one of the best ways to go out of this world: One minute you're in a $25 million jet fighting for your country, and the next minute you're in a ball of flame. It's instant. I can't think of a much better way to go than that."

Alan shook his head, remembering. "Then Mike just kinda smiled. You know his smile." Of course, I knew well the way it made you feel his ready acceptance, no matter who you were. That little gap between his two front teeth told you he wasn't flawless, symbolizing his humanity. Even now the echo of his laughter sometimes catches me by surprise. It conjures up a visual memory of smile lines spreading upward to outline his eyes.

Years after moving to Denton, Texas, Alan's family returned to Bartlesville for a visit and walked into the church. He didn't know if Mike would even remember him, but Mike was waiting. "I got something for you," Mike told him as he dropped butterscotch candies into his palm. That was just like Mike to remember Alan's favorite. Everyone he met was an individual, an important one.

When they met again they realized that even though Mike was a year younger, they both had pursued many of the same interests independently: playing cornet in the band, becoming drum major, getting a pilot's license, riding a motorcycle, buying a little car—Mike a Datsun 240Z, and Alan a 2-seater Triumph. Then Mike went Navy, and Alan was considering either Navy or Air Force.

During his senior year, Mike had vacation from the Academy, so they planned a ski trip. Early in the morning, while the others slept, Alan and Mike drove from Bartlesville to Denver in 11 hours. During the drive, they talked about the history of the Navy, women, politics, God, religion, motorcycles, scuba diving, and even the abundant life and their definition of that. Of course, they talked most about flying.

Memories of that ski trip flutter around Alan like so many birds. He recalls the throttle getting stuck wide-open—that always happened while going *down* the mountain. When they finally arrived back in Bartlesville late one night, the fireplace was blazing. The parents had retired. Alan slumped into a cozy chair listening to Denise and Mike talk, and the next thing he knew, he awoke in the chair, his boots having been pulled off and laid beside him. The comfort and joy of that time with Mike will always warm his memories.

Though they talked about taking a motorcycle vacation some day, Alan figured, as he had about the ski trip, that it was just talk. But Mike called months later, gave Alan some dates, and they made their plans. When Mike drove from Pensacola to Denton—1100 miles in 16 hours on his cycle—Alan realized what great physical shape he was in. Arriving about 2:30 in the morning, Mike ate a wonderful "breakfast" of cookies-and-cream ice cream with potato chips on top, Gatorade and cereal.

The next morning, deciding to suntan his legs, Alan pulled on his cut-offs and took off his shirt for the drive to Bartlesville. By the time they arrived, he was so burned he could hardly walk. Mike, of course, had a beautiful tan. Continuing on to Austin, Alan noticed Mike pull some index cards from his saddle bag, and later discovered they were Bible memory verses. "This guy even wanted to make God's Word a part of his vacation, while riding a motorcycle!" Alan said. "Neither of us ever said anything about it, but that spurred me on to do the same."

Whizzing through a small-town intersection, they failed to hear the sirens of an approaching fire engine above the roar of the motorcycles and nearly got creamed. A cop pulled them over.

"Did you hear the sirens?" he asked.

"No, Sir, we didn't."

"Did you know you're supposed to stop for emergency vehicles?"

"Yes, Sir, but we didn't know they were in the area."

"Well," he said, "just be aware to be aware."

"We thought that was lucky, and a clever saying, too, so the rest of the trip we reminded each other: Be aware to be aware," Alan laughed.

Arriving in Austin that evening, they set up their tent in the beautiful hill country with its mountains, lakes, rivers, and streams. Then they refreshed themselves at the Oasis Cantina. Twenty-seven levels of redwood decks are built down the side of the mountain, overlooking Lake Travis.

"We watched the sun go down, had some really good food and just kinda kicked back and talked. A beautiful sight," Alan remembered.

One theme of the trip was their common interest in women. They agreed that sometimes when they totaled everything about a woman, certain attributes canceled out her beauty. One night they devoted two and a half hours to listing the qualities of a beautiful woman. There, beside the campfire with s'mores and Coke, they wrote their qualifications for the *righteous fox* [Appendix 12]. "We just had a blast with that! It was good to focus on what we were looking for!" Alan said. Aside from Mary Ruth's reaction, it typified Mike's boyish sincerity and determination to find the best. True to form, the list embodies perfection.

Alan recalled with melancholy nostalgia the day he and Mike parted after that motorcycle trip. They just waved and separated, Mike heading back toward Florida, and Alan to Denton, Texas. That was a sad trip home for Alan. Not that he had any idea about the future, he just didn't want it to end. It had been perfect. In spite of Alan's speeding ticket, they both made it home safely. Of course, he never dreamed what he was speeding away from, and into, but of this he was certain: They had a future. There would always be that.

Mike and Alan began to plan their next adventure. They had skied and cycled, so the next trip would be to fly cross-country. While waiting, they once flew their dates to Dallas to hear Bill Cosby and another time Alan rented a plane, figuring he was on his own turf.

He may be Mr. Navy Pilot, but I have the experience of MY airplane. I'll be able to show him something—this'll be great. Mike will be sitting in the right seat while I'm the pilot this time. But within a few minutes, never having been in that plane before, Mike was flying it better than Alan's instructors. "He pulled chokes, touched buttons and did some beautiful work. It freaked me out," Alan recalled. "I realized then: *That guy was born to fly!*"

Yet another time Mike fiddled with the auto pilot. "Hey, man, don't mess with that thing. I don't think it works!" Alan warned him, his anxiety rising with the elevation. Mike continued to punch buttons while Alan continued to reprimand him, expecting to drop out of the sky. "You don't mess with a plane at 7000 feet," Alan said. Moments later Mike had them heading on a direct course on autopilot. "Yeaaah, Buddy!" Mike laughed.

Mike's physical acumen impressed Alan during a full day of waterskiing on Lake Texoma. His body fat was 6 percent. He was in excellent condition. They simply could not knock him down. He'd go non-stop until it was time to give the other three their turns. Finally, when the three couldn't take any more, they pulled the boat up and flopped exhausted on the beach. Looking up, they saw Mike—jogging.

Soon after, Alan wrote Mike he was engaged to Linda. They had talked to each other about Lenore and Linda, but not about getting engaged or married. Mike wanted to hear all about it. As Alan told him, "Well, she's on our righteous fox list. Check. Check. Check."

"Yeah," Mike said, "she's definite wife material." He told Alan he'd done well, and agreed she'd made the list. But he still wondered how to arrive at that big decision for himself. Alan explained he'd known her a long time and that she was the kind of woman who stays in the back of your mind even if you break up or put distance between you. Linda wasn't someone he could just forget. The situation either required something serious, or blowing it off for good.

"But it wasn't something that I wanted to blow off," Alan explained. Mike understood. He, too, felt a sense of loss that plagued him when he wasn't with Lenore. They agreed it was silly to go on looking and dating when someone on the list was right in front of you. Then came the day Alan met Lenore.

Planning to help her move from Arizona to Tennessee, Mike and Alan arranged to meet Lenore and her dad in Dallas. They would meet at a major intersection at 3 A.M. No one there. They had no way to contact them, so, by 9 o'clock that morning after a night of endless circling and looking, Alan was greatly agitated. Mike told him to calm down, that they had just pulled over to sleep. And sure enough, that's what had happened.

Finally connecting by calling Alan's home, they headed out to meet them again, but when Mike and Alan arrived at the designated location, there was no exit there. With no idea where they'd be in that whole city of Dallas, they got lost and drove for hours while Lenore and her dad were doing likewise. When they finally connected again by calling Mike's mom, they discovered Lenore was sitting at a pay phone about two blocks away.

That was the day Alan met Lenore. Her beauty and intelligence intimidated him. She was the kind of woman who knew what she wanted. Considering their list, he concluded, "Yeah, Mike, she may be it, all right."

Once Mike had plunged into marriage plans, too, Alan was excited about being a groomsman for Mike. Then he received a letter. Postmarked eight days before Mike disappeared, it raved about Lenore, about flying, about the mountains he flew over and about the F-18. He asked Alan if he would leave the wedding reception about fifteen minutes early to do pre-flight inspection and preparation on the plane Mike had rented for their get-away.

"Ahhh." Alan's drawl slowed down even more. He seemed almost stuck in neutral, not wanting to go on with his story. But slowly he eased into it. Grasping little insignificant facts to build on, he continued. "It was kind of strange that on Wednesday, on May 20, I was out on our front porch early in the morning, just looking at how beautiful the world was out there. Suddenly I called to Linda, 'We have to go flying.'"

Strange thing to say, strange thing to do in the middle of the week in the morning. Alan could not dismiss the extraordinary compulsion that prompted him to fly on that day, at that time. He checked the airport. A plane was available. He booked it. As they flew, they talked about Mike.

At that precise time, Mike, too, was flying—over the Sierra Nevada mountains that he loved. "We were right up there where he was," Alan said. "Flying together. Flying on Wednesday . . . "

It wasn't until the next evening that Alan's mother called to tell him that there was bad news about Mike. "I remember being bolted to that chair when she hung up," he said. "I remember crying. Shocked. Disbelieving. Overwhelmed. I thought: *There is no way. This is not something that happens to me. This obviously is not anything that could happen to Mike.* I knew Mike. I knew he'd never mess up. He doesn't make mistakes in an airplane. I couldn't believe it. This is a perfect jet—the F-18 Hornet, a $25 million piece of equipment—and there's nothing wrong with Mike. What could have happened?"

Then his thoughts switched to Lenore, to Don and Naomi, Denise and Nadean. "I imagined what they must be going through. That was a rough night for me. I cried and cried and cried. I woke up crying. A rough night turned into a rough day. A rough day turned into a rough week. Then it got to where I had good and bad days. I had a lot of questions. For God. I just didn't understand it. A nice guy like that, engaged to marry in a few more weeks! I couldn't believe God could allow something like that to happen."

One Sunday morning soon afterward, Alan found himself in church, another rough experience. While trying to sing a hymn that said something about God not sparing his own son, Alan felt like a ton of bricks were being thrown at him, one at a time. Cringing with each hit, he slumped into the seat, then rose to leave, weeping. He cried all the way home.

"I couldn't get those words out of my head. I saw the sacrifice of God giving up his own son in a new way. I saw for the first time what God really gave up for us—his own son."

Alan asked himself what Mike would want him to do at a time like that. The answer came coincidentally. He regularly called Don and Naomi who were staying at Mike's apartment in California by that time. One night they just handed the phone to Lenore. They didn't really know each other, but they became close friends in the ensuing weeks. Each day Alan called to talk about the events of the day, the searches, their feelings. Lenore was more of an encouragement to him than he was to her.

"Maybe that's why I kept calling," he said. "I wanted to believe Mike was alive. Maybe we could bring him back. Maybe together we could do it." Both a sense of hope and a sense of loss invaded him. He felt exposed. There was nothing he could do about it, so he just waited with everybody else. Totally vulnerable. Totally helpless. Then, Don's call came.

"Alan," he asked, "would you like to hike into the Sierra with me to look for Mike?"

CHAPTER 12

SEARCHING THE HIGH SIERRA

The Lord will provide . . . on the mountain,
it will be provided.
—Genesis 22:14

Clearly, if the military could not find them, Don must. His first attempt was with Bob Stonoff, Mike's would-be father-in-law. A high school biology teacher for 29 years, Bob also taught survival training. Highly qualified, his help was indispensable. He knew of pilots who had crashed and appeared even six months later. If the men were alive, time was critical.

They backed every effort with research and prayer. Their hopes high and urgency heightened, the two men first drove to the Mono Lake area in California. They licked dust while traversing dirt roads surrounding the nuclear testing site in Beatty, Nevada; Connie had described its shape on the map under hypnosis. They hiked, climbed, camped, and flew over the White Mountains and Black Mountains at the north end near Boundary Peak and the Chalfant Valley. But they learned nothing.

In 1869, John Muir wrote of the Sierra in *My First Summer* before planes disturbed her majesty's quiet: ". . . what glorious landscapes are about me, new plants, new animals, new crystals, and multitudes of new mountains . . . towering in glorious array along the axis of the range, serene, majestic, snow-laden, sun-drenched, vast domes and rivers shining below them, forests, lakes, and meadows in the hollows, the pure blue bell-flower sky brooding them all . . ."

More than a hundred years later, Don learned from Bob about the region's edible flowers and plants, savored the clear, blue streams at high elevations and wrote about those mountains and about what happened to him there. Excerpts from his prayer journal during his first week of searching reveal an equally awesome journey of a father, a spiritual giant who wrestled with the ultimate as he searched for his elusive lost son:

Tuesday, 23 June 1987

> Lord, this is a cool crisp morning here outside Bridgeport, California. I've been praying and crying to you as I looked at the beautiful High Sierra Mountains with the Bridgeport Lake in the foreground. The mountains are beautiful, but there is a bittersweetness to them. They are "more" or "less" beautiful, but something is foreboding about them . . . could it be those very mountains that took our Mike to you? And yet, let me not blame the mountains, for if he is with you, it wasn't the mountains that took him . . .
>
> Lord, I surrendered him to you this morning—to take or to leave. I sobbed at the thought of our loss. But wow! . . . As Paul said—to die is gain. Naomi and I used to sing, "Whatever it takes to be more like you, that's what I'll be willing to do," and, "Whatever it takes for my heart to break, that's what I'll be willing to do." Lord, I really didn't have quite this much in mind. This wasn't an option for you to choose. Yet, if we really meant it, we should allow for you to do as you will. If we didn't mean it, we shouldn't have sung it. How often do we say, sing,

or think things in such a shallow and meaningless way? . . . Lord, as Bob and I leave this "wonderful" mountain, allow us to have your presence and special discerning spirit to know just where to search today . . . Amen.

Wednesday night, 24 June 1987

Today we went to the Virginia Lakes and hiked up the mountain to about 11,000 feet, between Mono Lake and Bridgeport . . . As we reached the summit, I thought the other side would just descend as did the side we had climbed. But, wow! They were truly awesome, as Mike would say. There were peaks and ridges, canyons and valleys and lakes as far as we could see. It gave me a new love and fear of them. Where could we start? It gave me a discouraged feeling as I thought of the vastness of the places Mike might be. If Mike is gone, I'd rather he went with the plane than suffer for weeks in these mountains.

Lord, you know how much I want Mike back. I wish I could really believe and know he is still with us, but it's getting harder every day. If he is still here, Lord please continue to protect, feed, and care for him . . . We want to be reunited with Mike. I don't want to be selfish, Lord, but things just won't be the same without our only son. Bless Naomi, the girls, and Lenore tonight, and the coming days as we face the uncertain and unknown future. Amen.

Don could not have imagined just how "uncertain and unknown" the future would continue to be. After the families returned from California following the military memorial service, and after all air search efforts were suspended on June 2 with no clues worth pursuing, he could scarcely concentrate on anything but Mike. On the two-month anniversary of Mike's disappearance Don was back in Bartlesville, still waiting, still writing his thoughts to God.

* * * * *

Waiting it out finally convinced Don to plan the second, more intensive search with six men, including Don, Lenore's father Bob, Bill Bufford and John David from Bartlesville, Mark Crum from Visalia, California, and Alan. At last Alan would search for his missing buddy.

Not anyone you'd want to cross, Bill was the kind who could eat nails for breakfast. John, too, was "a good 'ole boy and really nice," Alan drawled. Both Vietnam vets, they were in top physical condition and folded Alan under their wings. Naomi's nephew Mark complemented the team. Bob appeared with his jaw swollen and purple, having just had oral surgery. Alan wondered how he'd ever make the trek, not realizing he should wonder how he himself would make it.

Based on the military information that Raider 58 had turned south before it disappeared off radar, Bob and Don set up the search for King's Canyon south of the LKP. Bob's experience as a survival trainer added to the excitement. Items that Alan would not have known to bring appeared magically, including walkie-talkies, a coffee pot, a gun. After eating their last good breakfast for nine days, Alan listened to them talk about the bear and rattlesnake count.

"I was ready to tear into those mountains," he exclaimed. "Just rarin' to go." He'd find Mike. He just knew it. "Well, I made it about 30 feet," Alan laughed at himself. "I was just exhausted." Having examined the maps and scale model of the area, he knew they had started on an easy trail. Bob reminded them they would experience even greater exhaustion at higher elevations.

"So, we kept going. And rested. And kept going. And rested . . ." Deer joined them. By nightfall, terror gripped Alan as he scaled the steep trail with a sheer drop-off on the left and rocks on the right. After feeling their way for unending hours in the dark, Alan longed to lay down his increasingly heavy pack.

Finally they stumbled into a flat area next to a body of water. Some scouted for firewood; someone built a fire and put the coffee pot on; others tried to read the directions on packets of dried food. Famished, they finally tore into the packets and dumped in some water, but they paid for their haste by ending up with raw rice and hard potatoes. "Then we got very crowded in the tent and zonked out," Alan said.

With the dawn, a cold chill sliced through their sleeping bags. Watching the sun rise over the ridge of a majestic mountain, they saw they had camped at the edge of Monarch Lake. After eating "weird oatmeal" that made him sick, Alan drank coffee to warm up. Wired like a spurt of jet fuel, he jumped up to follow the men up the steep gravel Sawtooth Pass—a killer of a climb.

Before long, days and nights blurred into a succession of hopes and dreams, disappointments and tears. Their emotions skyrocketed and plunged with the terrain as they worked and searched, prayed and laughed—as they did the night Don burned up Bob's pants while attempting to dry them by the fire.

One incident etched the image of a searching father into Alan's memory forever. After staggering into a clearing one night and sliding his backpack to the ground, Alan felt it must weigh as much as he did by that time. Not only was he physically exhausted, but also the load he carried inside was even heavier. Feeling unable to move another inch, he dropped onto a rock, stretched out, and closed his eyes. Another day had dissolved with no sign of Mike. No clues. Nothing. Hopelessness seeped into every cell. He could feel himself giving up on ever finding Mike.

Then, drifting into his hazy consciousness, he heard a strong and steady voice calling. "Mike? Miiiiiike!" He opened his eyes to see Don circling their camp. "I was too exhausted to move," Alan said, "but Mike's dad paced around us methodically, calling his son's name. His desperation and love wouldn't let him quit like the rest of us."

Alan groaned and shut his eyes again, then opened the floodgate to his tears. The driving force that empowered Don with unending stamina and energy stunned him. "What a man he is! Getting into those mountains and just being with Don did me a lot of good. To see in action the love of a man for his son. To watch him climbing and calling for him. To observe him physically burdened every day, every step weighted with love. To be in prayer as a group of men searchers, and then to see Don quietly turn his back to everyone and just cry—real hard . . . That did something to me," Alan spoke reverently. "I'll never get over it."

Lying there on that rock that night, Alan considered what it would be like to be a father. The love of a God who gave up a son awed him. He tried to fathom the loss of families whose children are kidnapped, or are MIA's and POW's. *Missing! Lost!* The words burned into his consciousness like molten lava.

Pictures of Mike drifted through his thoughts like poufs of clouds across a summer's sky: skiing on Colorado slopes; snorkeling in the gulf; eating ice cream for breakfast; baking yeast rolls; cycling through an intersection in a small Texas town, just missing a fire truck; flying with Prince Philip of Monaco; playing in the Drum and Bugle Corps for President Reagan's inauguration; scuba-diving and sailing; parachuting and flying. "How alive Mike still is to me!" he thought.

Days later when Don left his hopes of finding his son on the mountain, Alan remembered Abraham's willingness to sacrifice his son—also on a mountain. "I will provide," God had said. God saw what Abraham could not. Like Abraham, Don believed that God would provide—for Mike, for him.

* * * * *

Marilyn Ginsberg planned to visit her family in New York before taking the next step. She told Naomi before leaving Lemoore, "You have such great faith. I wish I had that faith, too." God was already at work to fulfill her desire. A

Christian man on the flight had prayed specifically for a seatmate to whom he could witness about his life-changing faith. But the seat was empty.

When Marilyn's children fell asleep, she moved to an unoccupied seat so the children could stretch out on those assigned to her. She soon found herself telling her story to a stranger, committing herself to a new relationship with God.

While in New York, her casualty assistance commanding officer (CACO) informed her they had again discontinued searching. Declare him *missing* or *dead*, the DOD told her, as though her choice might change the outcome. She declared him *presumed dead*. Ginsberg's death certificate arrived, a white paper no more impressive than an application or a questionnaire. *Place of death: in or near Glass Mountain*, she read. But, she thought: *The plane is still missing. What do they know?*

Then, the surprises began. Lenore called Marilyn with breakthrough information from a civilian: a *revised* last known position (LKP). It targeted the vicinity south of Bridgeport, northwest of Mono Lake. Immediately Marilyn called the Executive Officer (XO) who was unaware of any revision. He found that someone had forgotten to inform him. *Forgotten to inform him . . .*

She returned to Lemoore just before Lenore's trip to Bartlesville for Mike's memorial service on the wedding weekend and requested a renewed search based on the revised LKP, advanced technological assets to find the supposed wreckage and a copy of the JAG report. Angry, the commander told Marilyn he had instructed squadron personnel not to discuss the JAG report with the families. "Please do not put them on the spot by asking questions," he said. "Of course," he reassured her, "there is nothing in the report that you don't already know. It's just the principle of the matter." He agreed to arrange a NASA C-130 with earth resources palette and a helicopter with magnetic anomaly detection (MAD).

Disappointments continued to plague the families during that tortuous summer. On July 20, two months after the men disappeared, the second air search was initiated, but the Navy did not employ either the NASA plane or the MAD helicopter. Depressed and grieving over the possible loss of her husband, Marilyn continued to believe the Navy would find the plane any day. "I trusted them wholeheartedly," she said.

Then, she noticed a change—not suddenly, as a lightning flash of insight, but slowly, like a mass of clouds gathering. By September she began feeling impatient with the Navy's promises. "I had begun to accept the likely possibility of Dan's death, but the thought of never finding the plane and never having any answers was really getting to me," she said.

* * * * *

The search for Mike and Dan was yet embryonic. But Lenore and the families did not know that. Weeks folded over on themselves until they became months. By the time the first winter snows blanketed the Sierra Nevada on November 6, Marilyn momentarily gave up hope of finding the plane. After more than five months, all she had were letters of condolence from the President and the Admiral, and unending, seemingly unanswerable questions.

But again new information surfaced. Late that November, Marilyn read—was not told—that the Navy and Marine Corps had ordered 250 of the 384 active F-18 Hornet fighter jets grounded [Appendix 3]. 250 of them! Uncontained titanium fires in the engines were blamed for three crashes and suspected as the cause of a fourth that occurred that very week, in jets assigned to the USS Coral Sea and the USS Midway.

The media reported *no pilots* had been killed in any of the crashes and that the problems first became apparent in May, 1987. Had there been any other F-18 crashes in May of 1987?

What had happened in the same month that Raider 58 disappeared that indicated the F-18 was having problems? Or, if they were referring to Dan and Mike's plane, thus assuming the pilots were still alive, why hadn't they told the families about it? Why hadn't Marilyn heard that news, or about the revised LKP, when she had been in daily contact with the Navy through the long summer?

Collecting her questions and her composure, Marilyn called CDR Torrence to discuss it. "It's ridiculous to assume that current reports might be related to the mishap. If Raider 58 had an engine fire, Mike and Dan would have made a distress radio call. The fact that no call was made proves they impacted without prior warning," he said.

"But," Marilyn argued, "why does the Navy assume *pilot error* based on no warning?" She quivered under his resentment and hostility. In an emergency, protocol is: *aviate, navigate, communicate*. Of course, the pilot may not recognize the problem or its implications until it is too late to initiate corrective procedures. If an engine fire occurs, the emergency procedures take about 20 seconds to complete in a single seat F-18 Hornet, but may take 30-45 seconds in the event an IP is instructing the front-seat student pilot. If a pilot knows a crash is imminent and realizes that survival is not possible, he or she would probably attempt ejection rather than make a radio distress call. Of course, even though they are programmed not to panic, some most certainly do.

From early December through late January, Marilyn again remained on Long Island, New York, with her family. It gave her a reprieve to think about the circumstances surrounding the incidents. She had thought the F-18 had a perfect safety record. Still believing the Navy had not looked at this particular mishap with an open mind led her to a dedicated commitment to find the plane on her own. She could not have calculated the length of time or opposition that lay ahead. But before moving on with her life, she needed to do everything within her power to find her husband.

An attorney expert who had been counsel for McDonnell-Douglas which manufactures the F-18 Hornet, found it hard to believe that an F-18 was missing within the contiguous United States without either finding it or continuing to search for it. Three other attorneys told her: Without the wreckage, we can do nothing. Then an F-18 pilot who had participated in both the initial and second military searches studied the JAG report. He was shocked to discover the LKP was not near Glass Mountain. He had never heard otherwise.

In February, the Marine Corps informed Don and Naomi that another concentrated search was planned for the spring of 1988 as a training exercise, much like the July effort had been. The Muellers sent a copy of the letter to Marilyn, who was elated and called CDR Alexander to ascertain what types of aircraft had been used previously, and to request information on areas already searched to avoid overlap. He said the letter was misleading. They would not conduct another formal search, but he said she could request a similar SAR training exercise.

There were other means. Marilyn said she would either fund a search privately or request public funds from her senator. The commander responded sarcastically, "I would *hate* to see you contact a politician and request further searching. That would be a waste of time, energy, and tax payers' dollars." Soon after this conversation, on the pretense of concern for her emotional well-being, two chaplains appeared at her door. Hurriedly by-passing the supposed purpose of their visit, they questioned her about her plans for a search and asked for the names of the senators. CDR Whitten was finally assigned to help Marilyn publicize her own search.

In exasperation with the persistent widow's attempts to find her husband herself, officials told Marilyn to submit a list of specific questions to the Public Affairs Office at NAS Lemoore. Though personnel did not take the wife of CAPT

Ginsberg seriously, they should have known better than to think they could pass off her numerous "little requests and questions" by having her list them for a Public Affairs Officer. In response, Marilyn received a terse phone call in late March to inform her the NAS would schedule a briefing, her questions being "more numerous and in-depth than expected."

Eleven months after the plane had disappeared, Marilyn and the two fathers of the missing pilots attended the briefing intended to answer the families' questions. Held at NAS Lemoore, it was a formal gathering with assigned seating for the 35-40 Navy personnel and 3 family members. They were given copies of written material summarizing information that the families were told had already been given to them. Then, blow after blow stunned Marilyn and the fathers.

A Navy spokesperson began by telling the three that "practice sessions" for the briefing took approximately three hours, so they could expect to be there at least that long. Practice sessions? They were given pencils and pads and told to write down any questions rather than interrupt the presentation. The officials presented a lengthy, well-organized brief that stressed how much money and how many man-hours the search had consumed. Of course, these had not been among their questions.

At one point, Marilyn interrupted vehemently when CDR Torrence presented information to prove that Dan and Mike had made their last radio call at least 5-7 minutes after they had disappeared from radar. The courageous, strong, supposed widow explained that according to evidence she had gathered, Dan and Mike had made that radio call immediately prior to disappearing from radar. She firmly believed the plane went down at the point it vanished and asked whether they had considered that possibility and thoroughly searched *that area*. CDR Torrence answered that they had made the best educated guess possible, that the area had been thoroughly searched on numerous occasions, and that the plane was not there. Period.

When Don stretched his prerogative to ask about the possibility of a cover-up, the admiral, obviously resenting the question, flatly denied it and steered the briefing back to the formal presentation without allowing further opportunity to ask questions, or to discuss those that Marilyn had submitted earlier, or to open dialogue. By 7 P.M., everyone rose to leave, except three stunned, exhausted family members who still clutched their questions and confusion.

In spite of an increasingly perplexing agenda, Marilyn's vision and energy returned. She began the long, tedious process of organizing her own search in the Sierra Mountains. She devoted herself to researching, making hundreds of phone calls, reading numerous books, consuming innumerable hours interviewing, thinking, planning. Marilyn designed reward posters, maps, letters, and other relevant information to include in publicity packets, assisted by CDR Whitten.

In spite of official resistance, Marilyn insisted on offering a reward for information leading to the site. Then, CDR Whitten insisted on highlighting on the publicity map the area of highest probability for success in locating the plane: north of Bridgeport. This in spite of the fact that the front-seat pilot in the plane that followed Raider 58 said his first estimate of the plane's position was in error and verified that the missing F-18 had never gone farther than the *actual, revised LKP.*

So, the supposed widow continued feeling like someone lost in a maze that goes nowhere and yet expending great energy looking for a way out. On May 15, 1988, Marilyn mailed the search packets with a poster that offered a five thousand dollar reward for location of the plane [Appendix 9].

Like lighting the end of a stick of dynamite, the packets ignited a quicker response than anyone could have anticipated.

CHAPTER 13

KAVANAUGH RIDGE

For the Lord is the great God,
the great King above all gods.
In his hand are the depths of the earth,
and the mountain peaks belong to him.
—*Psalm 95:3-4*

A map with a surprise revelation from the Nevada Wing Civil Air Patrol (NWCAP) arrived in response to Marilyn's search packet. A scribbled note, that really did not have to be added at all, stated they had searched the area outlined on the map following the mishap in May of 1987 *because a witness reported hearing a crash in that area on May 20.*

Witness? Crash? Specific area? The day they disappeared? An adrenaline surge kicked Marilyn into action. She contacted the person who sent the note. That led her to Deputy Hysell from the Mono County Sheriff's Department in Bridgeport. A camper had indeed reported hearing a strange sound, perhaps an impact, on the day the men disappeared, and Hysell had advised the authorities. As neither the witness nor the sheriff was contacted by the Navy that year, they believed that the plane had been recovered.

One year later when the Sheriff's department received the search packet in the mail, they realized the missing plane had disappeared within three miles of the sound reported by the witness. Shocked to hear it had not been located, Deputy Hysell immediately asked the Forest Service for the wilderness permits for the year 1987. What he got was a lot of work: More than 10,000 permits were filed for the Green Creek Canyon area in 1987. They began calling everyone who had camped there on May 20th and eventually found the auditory witness.

Marilyn immediately called Richard Brown, the attorney in San Francisco who had heard the sound coming from the direction of Kavanaugh Ridge. Brown told her the weather had been pleasant with no indication of bad weather until early afternoon. His family was snowed in that night and could not hike out until May 22, at which time he reported the incident to the Forest Service. The person to whom he reported it told him the plane was already recovered.

Waiting for the Navy's response to the discovery of a witness, excitement quickened Marilyn's pulse and energized her activity. It looked like the plane would finally be recovered one year to the day of the mishap. When the Navy did not call, she contacted CDR Whitten. "Well, who told you about the auditory witness?" he asked, like that was the crux of the matter.

"So you *know* about a witness and didn't tell me?" she demanded.

"Calm down," he advised. "Just because a witness alleged he heard a crash doesn't mean the plane was even near that spot." He discussed pedantically the manner in which sound ricochets deceptively in the mountains. Amazed at his cool response, Marilyn told him the witness seemed certain of the direction from which he heard the sound. She requested he authorize search aircraft to be sent to that area as soon as possible. "That will take time to request and organize," the commander said. So again Marilyn waited, if somewhat impatiently.

On the night of the anniversary of the disappearance of Raider 58, CDR Whitten informed Marilyn that Fallon NAS had sent a helicopter to the area earlier that day. The pilot reported a heavy snow cover and had seen nothing.

"What's next?" Marilyn asked.

"Nothing," he replied. "As I said, the Navy knew about the reports of crash sounds in the Green Creek Canyon area last year and CAP ground teams already searched on foot." Dumbfounded, Marilyn gasped, "The Navy knew about a witness and a likely crash site, and searched there a year ago and didn't tell me?" Ignoring her incredulity and dismissing her queries, he calmly said, "Clearly, it does not make sense to search there again."

Marilyn gave up. Organizing her own search party was still the only reasonable option. The families supported her efforts. Back in Bartlesville on May 20, the one-year anniversary of Dan and Mike's disappearance, Don wrote:

> Bless the Lord, O my soul, and all that is within me . . . My heart wants to praise you, [yet] I ask: When, Lord? One year ago today, everything was as usual: Big expectations of that upcoming wedding day, no problems or troubles. What a year this has been . . .

Marilyn first secured firm commitments for assistance from individuals and groups. The NWCAP planned an air and ground search June 18-20, 1988. The Bay Area Mountain Rescue Unit (BAMRU) pledged fifty experienced hikers to search in July. But rules and bureaucracy threatened to cancel the efforts: lack of permission to go into a wilderness area; lack of support from the military to airlift the ground searchers into the mountains; complaints by the California CAP because the Nevada CAP was searching in California.

Then CDR Whitten called Marilyn with a surprise suggestion that he contact the Marine Corps Mountain Warfare Training Center (MCMWTC) in Bridgeport to request volunteers to participate. Elated that the Navy was cooperating with her efforts, she scheduled to meet the Marine volunteers on June 18 and 19.

The media publicized the plans in response to Marilyn's search packets. One news reporter uncovered rumors at Lemoore NAS that the missing aircraft had already been found by the Navy. An anonymous caller told Marilyn the Navy had found the plane shortly after the mishap. Would it never end?

On June 17 Marilyn drove to Bridgeport, the Mono County seat, for the search she had planned and arranged. She would finally meet LT Padilla and Deputy Hysell of the Sheriff's Department and Major Rushmore of the NWCAP. Together they would plan the next two days. Early in the morning on June 18, they all met at Bryant Field in Bridgeport: 10 planes from the NWCAP, each with a 2-man team, 5 on the NWCAP ground team and 20 from the MCMWTC. The Marines divided into 5 groups of 4 men each, one including an officer.

One by one the planes lifted off from the landing strip at the edge of Bridgeport and headed toward the Green Creek Valley in the Hoover Wilderness area and Kavanaugh Ridge where Richard Brown had reported hearing an impact a year earlier.

With the search underway, Rushmore, Padilla, Hysell and Marilyn talked as they waited for word from the searchers. Their conversation rumbled with revealing information. Each one raised questions and learned new answers. Marilyn expressed her suspicion of a malfunction with the plane. She told the men she was puzzled by the failure of the Navy to mention a witness.

Lt. Padilla agreed and added his own observation. "It seems strange that none of the Navy personnel that I spoke with about the incident ever mentioned that the plane went off radar in my jurisdiction."

"It's fascinating, too," said Deputy Hysell, "that I saw a sky crane fly into Green Creek Drainage Area a few days following the mishap."

"You must be mistaken," Rushmore exploded with

shock. "I'm sure it wasn't a sky crane you saw. They're extremely expensive to operate, and they're not a search aircraft." He knew a sky crane to be a Sikorsky helicopter used to lift out pieces of debris from otherwise inaccessible areas.

"But it most certainly was a sky crane," Deputy Hysell insisted. "It approached and left the area in an unusual manner, closely accompanied by two UH-1's. Search aircraft usually spread out to cover a larger area."

They all realized the implications simultaneously. Recalling the events of that search a year earlier, Rushmore remembered the Navy's specific command to the NWCAP: *Stay north of Bridgeport for the first 3 or 4 days of the search.*

The four found themselves thinking the unthinkable. Marilyn still was not ready to accept the idea, but tentatively they began to explore accumulating indications that the Navy likely knew the crash site back in May of 1987. Concluding that the evidence seemed to imply that, they could only ask *Why?*

Like an explosion that is expected but still frightens the ones that are waiting, at approximately 2 P.M. a radio call came in from one of the ground teams on Kavanaugh Ridge. Strangely enough, Connie under hypnosis back in Bartlesville had attempted to name a place she saw: KAN . . . KAV . . . CAD . . . Could that possibly mean the discerners had been on the right track after all? Was Mike still alive on Kavanaugh Ridge?

The Marines had found tiny pieces of composite material they assumed were from an F-18 Hornet. Rushmore telephoned Lemoore NAS to inform them of the suspected find. They would send someone on Monday—two days later.

The Navy's nonchalance shook them as surely as an earthquake. The little waiting group did not trust the ground beneath them. The foundations of their trust in the Navy cracked and crumbled with each aftershock. But Fallon NAS did send a helo within the hour. Locating the ground team of Marines who had found the debris, they lifted them out and landed back at the Bridgeport airport.

The two helicopter pilots from Fallon had also been involved in the initial Navy searches. The commander in charge showed Marilyn and the others some of the pieces discovered. He confirmed they were F-18 material, but needed lab analysis to be sure it was the missing Hornet.

"We'll take over from here," the pilots informed Rushmore. "No one is to return to the area. You did a good job, Sir." Then they got into their helicopter and flew away. The volunteer Marines lingered. CAPT Miller, whose team found the first piece, considered it "simply luck" that the route covered by his search team took them almost directly to the crash site. They had begun their search approximately 3 miles northeast of Dunderberg Peak and they worked their way around the peak, through the saddle, and down a steep 2500 foot rock slide on Kavanaugh Ridge. It was while sitting at the base of the canyon to eat lunch that one of the team members found the first piece of the missing aircraft: a 1" by 4" piece of carbon/graphite material. Remarkable coincidence.

When a Navy helicopter lifted in to Kavanaugh Ridge the officers who served on the accident board, they found the actual impact site within 2 hours at 10,400 feet. The plane had impacted a 70-degree granite face at the top of the treeline with only one tree having been clipped prior to impact. They showed Marilyn a piece of molten metal they retrieved.

Falling rocks and dirt, similar in color to the exterior paint of the FA-18, covered the site. Thousands of small pieces of aircraft had rained across the ridge like hail from heaven. Each weighing less than 20 pounds, much of it was buried in loose rock and scattered in an area 1.5 miles horizontally by 1800 feet vertically. Due to extremely hazardous terrain, the helicopter hovered above a large boulder to allow MAJ Crew and CDR Lyle to jump the last two feet to the rock below. The drop-off point at the base of the slope was approximately 8500 feet above mean sea level. After climbing four hours, CDR Lyle reported he had only climbed about 800 feet vertically.

Over the next two weeks, they surveyed and excavated

the site. CDR Lyle reiterated the opinion of CAPT Miller that it was sheer luck that allowed them to locate the wreckage. Only after climbing the ridgeline for two weeks, and marking the impact site with a 6 x 6 foot piece of bright orange parachute material, was he able to locate the site from the air. "I flew over the site numerous times and saw no evidence of wreckage without the orange marker."

By July 6, 1988, the investigation was complete and the missing plane was identified. The left vertical stabilizer of an F-18 with the side number of 535 clearly in view was the largest piece found. The only part of the maintenance signal data recorder (MSDRS) that was found was the left side cover plate. An extensive search of the area turned up nothing else. The only other data storing units in the aircraft are the mission computers. Only extremely small pieces of these electronic components were found and no data could be recovered from them.

Driving back to her home in Hanford, Marilyn thanked God for the miracle. She confessed she had begun to believe that the plane would never be found. But the weather had been perfect, none of the searchers had been hurt, and pieces of the plane were found within seven hours of beginning the search after more than a year of waiting for the Navy to find her husband. That she was at first actually elated with the discovery of possible pieces of Dan's plane amazed her, but sadness soon overshadowed the joy as the reality and finality of Dan's death wrapped their tentacles around her thoughts, her heart, her future.

When she called the families, some reactions surprised her. The Stonoffs were astonished that Marilyn attributed the finding of the plane to God. They suggested the Navy could have arranged for her to "find" the plane as a result of her persistence and determination, because they had known its location for a year.

Initially rejecting that possibility, Marilyn nonetheless began to explore some pertinent questions. Seeds of doubt had been planted repeatedly. And they began to grow. Based on Richard Brown's expert witness, what if the fifty experienced SAR mountain climbers—civilians—had discovered the crash site outside the Navy's control when they had planned to search three weeks later? What if pieces of the aircraft were already missing? What if they found evidence of a fire or impact at a steep angle? Perhaps the Navy had no choice but to give the families what they wanted: a crash site.

When Don and Naomi heard the results of the search, they knew they had to go to Kavanaugh Ridge. For the third time, Bob Stonoff was the key man. He would climb with them to the crash site in August. They needed to bring closure to the likelihood of Mike's death. Nadean and Denise would join them for Mike's twenty-eighth birthday—on Kavanaugh Ridge.

Don and Bob had been within three miles of the site when they explored the northern section the first summer, and about four miles south of the site when they searched the Virginia Lakes area. The commander warned them it would be difficult to hike there. But a helicopter rented for $400/hour; it would take an hour both ways, plus search time, and landing was precarious. They next asked the Forest Service to lift them in, but without an emergency situation they could not assist.

Not to be paralyzed in their attempt, they discovered they could easily drive up the back side—the east side—of Kavanaugh in a land rover or Jeep, and then hike the rest of the way. But descending the west side, which is sheer granite at a 70-90 degree angle, would be hazardous.

Kavanaugh Ridge had been named after Stephen Kavanaugh who was employed to tunnel into a gold vein high on the ridge about 1900. On the first day, the six hiked for hours in the shadow of the impressively rugged ridge, approaching it from the west near East Lake. Even as the family gazed at Kavanaugh, they needed to get closer; they needed to explore Mike's mountain, to feel it beneath their feet and touch it with their hands. Still impersonal, the mountain compelled closer scrutiny the following day when they would attempt to reach the site.

The next morning, Mono County Deputy Sheriff Randy Hysell drove them up the east side of the mountain in the county's 4-wheel-drive Suburban. When the vehicle ran into snow, the six family members, including Bob and Mark, climbed by twos to the top of the ridge in 20 minutes. Then the challenge: a 90 minute descent down the west side of the mountain to the crash site.

Closer, still closer they struggled on, often slipping precariously. The adrenaline surge resulted not only from the physical challenge, but also from remembering the clairvoyants' visions of such scrubby brush and rock, and of Connie sliding all around the word *Kavanaugh* when trying to sense Mike's location. Their hearts quickened; their senses tingled. Closer and closer they struggled on.

They began noticing small chunks of man-made debris splattered randomly across the mountain. Such things did not belong there; they were definitely out of place. As their eyes adjusted to the reality of the moment, they saw thousands of small metallic chunks of F-18 all across the mountain. Then larger pieces loomed around them: the carrier tail hook in excellent condition appeared to be parked on the ridge flanked by wing pieces approximately 4 by 8 feet. They had been told there were no pieces larger than a man's hand. There were thousands of pieces of debris, but no clothing or identifiable body parts. That reminded them of the clairvoyants back in Bartlesville. "You won't find them there," they had said, "because they are not there."

Suddenly, Bob made a miraculous discovery: the plastic part of the key and ring for Mike's Honda cycle that he had ridden to Lemoore Naval Air Station more than a year earlier. Don's painful moment of truth on the mountain struck him like a lightning bolt. "I thought I'd given up on Mike's survival," Don said, "but that settled it. That clinched it for me." He turned his back on the others and tried on the words to see if they would fit: "*Mike . . . is . . . dead!*" he thought.

Sitting together on a level rock plateau with a sheer cliff dwarfing them, the six family members sensed an assurance more precious than gold. They affirmed their faith in God's sovereignty and their submission to God's will and purpose in Mike's likely death. They also asked questions. Looking toward the impact site, Bob asked, "Why couldn't he have been to the right, or four hundred feet higher?" Why indeed?

Don lay on that lofty rock gazing at the west side of Kavanaugh Ridge, considering his own questions. Why was Mike even headed that way? Where did Mike's precious body impact the earth? What happened to his body parts? How could they not find this place in all their searches? Did the Navy know within a couple of days? Did they take any body remains or aircraft debris out at that early date? Why did the mountain have to be there at all?

"It's easy to think of the mountain as a killer of our son," Don said, "but I accept God's purpose in all things. It's hard to understand, but I determine continually to believe: *As for God, his way is perfect.*" Don held Naomi as she wept, but her tears didn't last long.

"How wonderful to know God is in control," Don said. "How great God is!" Faith flickered, but never went out. Hope dwindled, but never disappeared. They saw beyond Kavanaugh Ridge.

Bob Stonoff, well-acquainted with the wilderness and the mountain, had brought his expertise and love for Mike to three searches. He poured his memories and feelings for his would-be son-in-law into *The Broken Wing.*

> On wings as an eagle, he rode the winds above the unending panorama of forest, meadows, and mountains. He soared above the Sierra's granite-crowned ridges and peaceful valleys—valleys carpeted in green and tacked down with yellow daisies—valleys whose walls were curtained with deep hues of pine, spruce, and fir, and splashed with the white of aspen—valleys whose walls

> were enhanced by silvery ribbons of tumbling, musical streams, and whose ramparts were adorned with Kodachrome spires of ancient rock . . .
>
> But alas, his wing is now broken, his strength has failed, and the pull of earth is heavy upon him as he reluctantly turns downward and plunges from his lofty realm to the world of reality and of time . . . The courage of his heart, his will to endure, his zest for life, his love for family and friends, his yearning for God, his desire to always mount up higher—all must crumble into dust—dust to mix with the elements of Kavanaugh . . . On new wings and with a stronger heart, he soars again . . . he climbs beyond the reach of the atmosphere and the earth's gravitational pull to race along the Milky Way, to loop beyond the farthest star—to sprint with the meteorites, and to soar— alongside of God—forever.

Like a train stopping at stations, each discovery on the mountain let some of us go. For some, finding the crash site clinched it; for others, it was the miracle of finding Mike's motorcycle key. For Don, learning that the ejection rockets had not ignited, and seeing the photos of the parachutes in the folded configuration proved they could not have ejected. Still others believed Mike was indeed gone when they saw his wallet, surely proof of his death even if remains were never discovered.

I was present when Naomi later handed the wallet to Connie. Carefully unwrapping the plastic cover, she laid it on the counter and slowly opened it, dirty and gritty, with one corner singed.

"When it arrived, it was still wet," Naomi told us. She and Don had separated the picture compartments carefully and laid them out under the ceiling fan to dry. The colors were blurred and images hazy, but they identified Mike and Lenore's engagement photo and a black and white picture of Mike and Gene. Seven dollar bills were still in perfect condition.

Connie gently rubbed her hand over it, the sandy grit sifting onto the plastic. "The fact that Mike's billfold was found doesn't confirm his death," she reasoned, "but just that their plane went down there." I was dumbfounded. And there began another journey: locating and identifying body remains. But surely that wouldn't take long. Surely the greatest silence had been broken; surely the longest wait was over. Lenore was not yet ready to experience the pain of seeing Kavanaugh Ridge where Mike's beautiful body had entered the earth in one final sacrifice. Even though she knew they found the crash site, this question still floated like a ghost to haunt her: *What if he isn't dead?*

Nadean, too, asked questions: How had the Christian discerners who had never known Mike all come up with the same, yet independent affirmations of Mike's survival and subsequent capture by a drug ring? Why did all of them continue to insist: *Mike is alive*—no matter what was discovered on Kavanaugh Ridge? Waiting for answers to the questions that still hung over them like a canopy of darkness, they could say to Mike in the words of Mark Crum:

> Come closer now and make known your presence. The grief has come and gone and come again. The longing of our voice pulls from within. Thoughts pour through, a shared moment, a well-traveled verse, a look—your look—we remembered.
>
> Our tears are for the present loss. Our joys are for the future reunion. We cry for what we no longer have. We take comfort in what will be. A reason, a question, an understanding of the inexplicable . . . The answer is God's answer. The reason is God's reason . . .

"I'd rather he'd be gone than go through this," Nadean confessed. "When they found pieces of an F-18, I felt relief. When I climbed to the site and saw the debris and then Mike's wallet and motorcycle key, that proved Mike is gone. I was ready to end it. But yet these women still insist: These *things* aren't Mike."

I could see that the search had not really ended on Kavanaugh Ridge. The pain in her voice, the tears on her cheeks, the pleading in her eyes wrapped me in sadness. The clairvoyants remained unconvinced. Even as Navy officials ridiculed the absurdity of believing in the survival of the pilots, just so intensely did the discerners rejoice in believing that Mike was still alive after ejecting. Connie still believed it. So did Bertha and Ann. As Betty told the Muellers, "Until I have proof, until they identify the bodies, I will not believe."

But there were no bodies.

CHAPTER 14

SIGNIFICANT SILENCE

When my prayers returned to me unanswered,
I went about mourning as though for my friend or brother . . .
O Lord, you have seen this; be not silent.
Do not be far from me, O Lord.
—Psalm 35:13b; 22

The secretive silence that shrouded what happened on Kavanaugh Ridge occluded the missing bodies, the Navy investigative reports and even the face of God. Too much was still hidden. The absence of vital information undergirded my own growing obsession to discover more.

I flew to Los Angeles where Patty and Wes Marquart, the parents of my friend Dave, loaned me the keys to their car and their cabin. Heading out of Orange County in southern California toward the desert on the east side of the Sierra Nevada, I would explore a world that aerial navigators miss.

Climbing steadily, I felt close enough to the mountain to touch it. Silver and seafoam green clumps of desert sagebrush dotted the sandy plains like so many French knots on oyster linen. Rabbitbrush and greasewood, tall, spiked surprises of brilliant blue lupine and squatting golden butterbrush hugged the edge of Interstate 395 that slices eastern California from Nevada.

California-bound adventurers had basked in the *gran sierra nevada,* first called so by Father Pedro Font, who was amazed by the grandeur of its snowy peaks. Stretching more than 400 miles long, and up to 80 miles wide, the Sierra is the longest mountain range in the contiguous United States and boasts the highest mountain peak, while only 85 miles away, Badwater in Death Valley is nearly 300 feet below sea level. From scorching desert sun to year-round snow pack, the Eastern Sierra reflects God's ongoing creativity.

The Marquart cabin on the June Lake Loop lies snuggled among ancient trees and rocks, lakes and sleepy volcanoes within a few miles of Green Creek Canyon at the foot of Kavanaugh Ridge. The generous provision of a cabin exactly where I needed it awed me. I was moving closer and closer to Mike.

A ranger and topographer who once lived within view of Kavanaugh, Fred Richter would be my guide. We would drive as far as possible until snow made the road impassable and from there hike up the east side of the ridge. Fred filled the distance with stories about Kavanaugh and the Eastern Sierra. He talked nonchalantly about the flora and fauna and geology on the way to Green Creek campground. Tall groves of aspen and Jeffrey pine rose and fell with the mountains and valleys. My excitement increased as the mountain loomed larger.

Fred and his friend Sally spread out our lunch by the creek. This was the quiet spot where Richard Brown had *not* heard the sound of a plane passing low-level directly over his head just prior to the crash. Campers always shudder when an F-18 interrupts the morning stillness of campfire coffee in Green Creek Canyon.

We began the drive up the back side of Kavanaugh Ridge on the dry, wide path snaking its way up the mountain. Suddenly, rounding a curve, there they were: snow drifts. Fred and I continued on foot, leaving Sally to play in the snow with her children.

Thinking I had prepared for the strenuous physical activity, I was surprised that the two and a half-hour climb made me feel I was ascending a never-ending stairway to the sky. Fred stopped often to offer me a drink, let me rest—and breathe— and to tell stories about rescuing people who thought they could climb mountains.

Snow cups, indentations in the snow, made each step one of calculation and design. They sometimes appear as deep as a couple of feet, though these were 8-12 inches deep and several inches in diameter. As we struggled up the terrain, Fred continually encouraged me by pointing out the next ridge, saying he thought that was the top. I kept on believing him.

At last he forged ahead, sure that we had arrived. I plodded on slowly. Fred grew smaller. The sky looked big and still far-away. Then I saw Fred waving both arms. He had made it! Minutes later, standing as close as I dared to the descending precipice on the west side of the mountain, I gazed both inward and outward. So this was it.

Tears washed over me. Fred waited respectfully. The tears came because I realized I missed Mike no more while gazing at that precipice than I do when I see him in other people—in Lance, in Don; or when I hear his laughter suddenly break in on a conversation, so real I turn to see him; or when I feel his hand on my shoulder in a dream, so real I awaken to touch him. I knew he would never really leave me, and that I would not leave him here on Kavanaugh Ridge.

Bev Hubbard Hage wrote this tribute to Mike and his mountain:

You died as you lived,
all out, full speed,
MACH 10.
Most get forty pounds of marble
Two feet high
Carved with name and date
Content to lay nestled in satin
Six feet below.

You rest at the base
Of a million pounds of granite
Thousands of feet high
Surrounded by the majestic
Artistry of the One you adored.

The high-speed impact
Carved your name and date
While scattering the perishable.
Temporal bones, wildly strewn
Mingled with the metal of flight.

Your soul is now free to soar
Through corridors of space
Laughing, exhilarated,
Racing through clouds
Unencumbered, immortal.

Fred climbed northward along the ridge to see what he could from that angle and offered to help me climb down the precipice into the area where the plane had impacted at 10,400 feet. But it was already mid-afternoon. Dark and cold come early to the Ridge. It had taken Don and the others 90 minutes to climb down to the site. I was close enough. To have discovered any debris from Raider 58 would not have helped. Only hurt. Yet, I was reluctant to leave. Towering peaks surrounded the valley below, Kavanaugh Ridge bordering the eastern side of the basin with other peaks standing at attention around this hallowed spot. East Lake, West Lake and Green Lake, set like three tiny jewels in the center of the valley, lay far beneath us at an elevation of approximately 8500 feet. Fred pointed out the highest peak in Nevada, visible on that clear day.

On the way down, a giant rabbit-like creature, almost kangaroo size, ran past us. Fred disappeared, chasing after it into the brush to identify it. Silence closed in around me.

Totally quiet, I felt eerie, unreal, alone. Not even Mike was close to me on the mountain. I had not found him there.

*****

The next morning I drove into Bridgeport. A pleasant kind of town, Bridgeport is the paradigm of small-town Americana, proud of its history and competent in its accomplishments. The dignified courthouse in this Mono County seat is California's oldest still in use. Nestled among hills ringed by mountains, its library and park, municipal offices and police station embody a people whose lives are shaped by the land. Life is not fast there, but it runs decent and deep.

It was in Bridgeport that Marilyn's search team met to fly into Green Creek Canyon and to the Ridge and where she had waited with others for their return. It was there that LT Padilla and Deputy Hysell would tell me their story about finding the auditory witness and assisting Marilyn's search. Generous with both information and time, they and their staff showed unusual interest in the men who had disappeared in their jurisdiction. Adjacent to the courthouse, the librarian Arlene Reveal welcomed me to her town, her mountains, her knowledge of history.

I spent the following day with Dave Marquart who works as a U.S. Forestry Service ranger at Mono Lake. He had heard about the lost F-18 in May of 1987. During the first months of searching, some thought that the lake held the secret to the missing men.

Walking on the lake shore with Dave, I viewed the volcanic Panum Crater, and Negit and Paoha Islands where hot springs bubble up, and learned about the courageous intervention by Sallie and David Gaines who had saved the lake from permanent destruction. Tall tufa towers created there by the highly alkaline deposits seem to guard the lake from those who would steal its water.

Approaching Dave's cabin at dusk, I knew his love for the flora and fauna of the Eastern Sierra was the kind about which John Muir wrote, Ansel Adams photographed, and for which David Gaines lived until his untimely death. Sitting in his low rope swing, I breathed in the night air enveloping the quiet utopia and gazed toward the sunset. Time stopped. I inhaled the fantasyland of beauty, and quiet, and peace. Written for just such moments, verses flowed like the quiet stream through my thoughts:

> "I will lift up my eyes unto the hills . . ."
>
> —Psalm 121:1
>
> "Going to the mountains . . . is going home . . ."
>
> —John Muir
>
> "Who can define the moods of the wild places?"
>
> —Ansel Adams
>
> "We need to see them with our hearts as well as our minds."
>
> —David Gaines

On the ten-mile drive back to his parents' cabin late that night, I pulled to the side of the road in awe. Mono Lake reflected the splendor of an orbiculate moon sailing the sky. Only God could have created such a perfect glimpse of the earth that Mike viewed just before he disappeared.

The next morning I swept the Marquart cabin clean, scooped up a rug to shake it outside, and pushed open the sliding glass door. There, as another pure gift, a rainbow washed the adjacent peaks in front of the cabin, draping its glory over them from the top to the valley floor. I took its promise of hope with me.

Setting out through Yosemite to visit Lemoore, the home of Squadron 125, fog and rain enveloped me. I was thankful, for to travel through such country as that without stopping to savor its majesty seems an obscenity. Geologists and poets, naturalists and historians, scientists and tourists, environmentalists and artists—without exception all who come take something of the mountains away with them. Or, perhaps what they take is hidden within them all the time, buried by layers of civilization and time constraints and obligations.

I finally understood why Mike longed to bring Lenore to the Eastern Sierra.

*****

Arriving at NAS Lemoore made me feel like a pest at best and a spy at worst. The walls built fast. Having called ahead for an appointment, I was surprised to find a change of attitude between the first and subsequent conversations. My purpose in visiting Lemoore was to talk with someone who might have known Mike, or at least to see the place where he last lived and worked. And just maybe, I might discover some clue to the mystery and secrecy.

The Public Affairs Officer said I should have arranged my visit several weeks in advance, that clearance was necessary through Washington, D.C., that an upcoming air show kept personnel too busy to see me, that Mike's squadron was out in the Pacific at the time, and so on. Not realizing that I was being put off, I had called Washington, D.C., at 5:30 the morning I left for Lemoore to facilitate clearance and discovered another strangely circuitous route. My call was switched from person to person. Finally, someone advised me that I did not need clearance to visit the Naval Air Station; he did not know why they were making such a big deal about my visit.

Relieved, though still puzzled when I arrived in the town of Lemoore, I stopped at the first gas station to call Allen Chambers, the Public Affairs Officer. Informed by a kind secretary that Mr. Chambers was in a meeting, I was told to call back in an hour. This process continued into mid-afternoon. Between phone calls, I found Mike's honeymoon apartment that he'd left on the morning of May 20. The door was ajar, and I pictured him locking the apartment for the last time, climbing on his cycle and driving into the California dawn.

Suddenly late Friday afternoon, panic struck me broadside. Mr. Chambers could end up leaving for the weekend and I'd miss him. Finally, greatly relieved, I was put through to Mr. Chambers who gave me the reason for the delay: "Ordinarily visitors don't need clearance, but it is different with you. I simply cannot give you permission to write a book about this mishap."

Permission! I didn't know whether to be amused or infuriated. I tried another approach. Letting him know I understood his workday was over, I explained I had traveled three thousand miles to see him and had been hanging out at the corner gas station for hours while waiting. Sympathizing with his intensely busy day (avoiding my calls, meetings, what-have-you), I asked him to meet me for as long as he had time to spare.

"Perhaps I could take you to dinner," I suggested. "Just name the place." I noticed I was beginning to beg. Afraid to wait for his answer, I finally told him that I really was not a spy, hoping that a sense of humor—or persistence—would work. Something did. At first defensive, Mr. Chambers observed that I was really quite harmless, and certainly neither Barbara Walters nor Agatha Christie. He then gave me an inside tour, a videotape about the F-18, a peek at the simulators—only a peek. Before leaving we walked outside onto the field dotted with F-18's. Parting on friendly terms, I had learned only that I knew more than he about the mishap that was now a fading memory for him. When he remarked that the widow was especially persistent, I asked him if he could appreciate why.

* * * * *

Early the next morning I drove into San Francisco to

interview the witness who had reported hearing the sound of an impact on Kavanaugh Ridge. After granting permission to tape the conversation, the attorney pressed the record button himself and stated that the interview was for press purposes only. His credentials amazed me. Of all the campers that might have been in the Green Creek campground on May 20, it had been Richard Brown. About 80 percent of the law he practices relates to aviation accident litigation; he was then serving on the plaintiff steering committee for the PAN AM 103 Lockerbee disaster, and was chairperson of aviation litigation for the Association of Trial Lawyers of America.

"The irony of this is that I like to get away from all that death and destruction and disaster by going camping," he said. But his trip to the Sierra Nevada the week of May 18, 1987, unexpectedly involved him in the kind of incident from which he sought a reprieve. One year later he noticed among his phone messages one that intrigued him: Call Randy Hysell from the Mono County Sheriff's Department. Thinking one of his law partners was playing a practical joke on him, since he had just returned from camping in the Eastern Sierra, he dialed the number fully expecting someone would accuse him of a "crime" in the area.

Instead, Deputy Hysell asked whether he had camped there. Brown told him he'd just returned. "Not now," the deputy said, "but a year ago, did you report hearing the sound of a possible aircraft impact?" Brown answered in the affirmative, but said he'd been informed that the plane was recovered.

"Well," the deputy said, "that was incorrect information. Although the Navy has given up on it, the pilot's widow has mounted an extensive effort to find the plane, and I'm looking for it at her request. We think you may have some information that would be valuable in locating the aircraft."

Telling Hysell he thought he could identify within a mile the direction the noise came from, Brown moved into action, his expertise showing. He said he would call Hysell back in half an hour. Richard Brown's office is two blocks from the headquarters of the U.S. Geological Survey on Battery Street. He sprinted there to get a topo map, marked the spot from which the sound came, and called the deputy in Bridgeport to give the coordinates.

"In no time they found the plane." Brown leaned back in his chair, sensing the interview was over, but I wanted more. After Marilyn's volunteers found the plane, Brown understood that the Navy implied *pilot error* caused the crash. But, being a well-practiced attorney, certain details bothered him.

"The most valuable piece of information that I had to give was that *there was no jet engine noise* associated with the impact, either before or after," he said. He leaned forward in his chair and stared straight into my eyes. His observation meant that, in the silent early morning, the thunderous engines passing almost directly overhead, were not running.

"And that's what was unique and strange about what I heard," he continued thoughtfully. "Of course, I expected the Navy to contact me." Knowing the importance of such a testimony in aviation accident investigation, Brown had requested from Marilyn the name and telephone number of the investigative officer at Lemoore NAS. "Strangely, he did not seem interested in what I was telling him," Brown recalled. Then the official dismissed him saying, "We'll get back to you and interview you when it's appropriate, and thank you very much." I asked whether the Navy had ever contacted or interrogated him. Brown shook his head slowly. To this day, no one has contacted this prime witness.

Remarkable. That the Navy did not approach him during the investigations shocked and dismayed me. Considering his expertise in aircraft mishaps, the Navy would have found his account to be especially valuable. Had they inquired a year earlier of the U.S. Forest Service or Mono County sheriff's office in Bridgeport, the witness would have led them to the site immediately.

Military accident investigations are closely controlled by the military. Rarely would anyone outside the military be consulted, except for manufacturers of the aircraft or component parts. "One of the ironies of these stories," Brown offered, "is that these men who risk their lives flying these high-powered machines can crash while the military sometimes hides the mechanical failures or failures of component parts to protect the defense industry."

Brown explained the same view that I found expressed by others, both civilian and military. A cover-up following an airplane mishap may be the result of the military's participation in the defense industry's investment. Rather than admit the manufacturer's culpability, it is far easier to cover up malfeasance in design of the plane with two simple words: *pilot error*.

The reasons for that are varied. It is no secret that numbers of aviators, Pentagon officials and others who work in military aviation eventually work for the defense contract industry. If an individual stirs up any degree of bad publicity or records of complaints against defense contractors, word gets around. "It's a small community," Brown said. "The revolving door between the aviation industry and the military works to the disadvantage of flight safety."

He reiterated the irony of the situation by contrasting fliers who risk their lives in these exacting jobs with those who happen to die in different circumstances. In one instance, a pilot may die in a crash in the Sierras as a result of mechanical failure or a maintenance problem. "That pilot likely gets blamed personally," he said, "and their families and children have to live with the specter that—there's no kinder way to say it—that they killed themselves."

And then there's the pilot who lives several years longer, engages in combat in the Persian Gulf war, and crashes—again as a result of mechanical failure or a maintenance problem. That pilot is honored as a hero. Of course, that makes a difference to their families, both in terms of military compensation and in personal acceptance. Not only do memorials and accolades honor those who give their lives in active duty, but also trust funds and civilian endeavors abound for their families. But there is no "widows and orphans fund" for military fliers killed in peacetime and training, even for identical reasons.

"It's a tremendous irony that Ginsberg and Mueller were killed and their families have to live with a black mark on their records," Brown continued, "when it could well have been the result of mechanical failure rather than pilot error. I know both military and civilian personnel in the National Transportation Safety Board who so easily blame the pilots if they either can't locate the reason, or do not want to expose it. That's the easy thing to do."

When Brown spoke of his admiration for Marilyn's tenacity in pursuing the truth, I told him I had just come from NAS Lemoore, and that they remember her, though not necessarily in a complimentary way, as one widow who wouldn't quit.

"Traditionally, the widow is supposed to accept what the CO says, shed a few tears, accept the flag and military benefits, and not be heard from again." He cited a convincing example of a group of widows who, like Marilyn, insisted that the U.S. and Canadian governments suppressed the real reason for the crash of a commercial DC-8 that was transporting multi-national troops of the 101st Airborne Division from Egypt to Ft. Campbell, Kentucky.

Finally, he pulled out an 8 x 10 enlargement of a photograph of Kavanaugh Ridge he had taken while hiking Green Creek Canyon that morning after having heard the sound of an impact. When I asked to make a copy for the Muellers, he said, "Please, give this picture to them."

When I told Lance Carr about my meeting with Richard Brown, he listened carefully and then asked me to affirm what I had told him.

"Did the witness, or did he not, hear the sound of a plane

before the impact?" Lance asked.

"There was no jet engine noise associated with the impact, either before or after. That's what is unique and strange about what I heard," Brown had told me.

"That," Lance said knowingly, "is significant."

Silence surrounded too many circumstances related to the mishap. Brown had indicated that even Raider 58 was silent just before it crashed. And the questions addressed to God, who knew all the answers we sought, remained unanswered. Not the least among the silent multitude was the Navy. We could not ignore the implications of the significant silence that wrapped itself like a furry coat around its mute and thickened tongue.

CHAPTER 15

DIGGING DEEPER

Whatever is hidden is meant to be disclosed, and
whatever is concealed is meant to be brought out into the open.
—*Mark 4:22*

The search had begun with two major questions: Where is the plane? Are Mike and Dan alive? Thirteen months later, two other questions obsessed the searchers: What caused the crash? Where are the bodies? Family members and friends felt themselves volleyed mid-air from one court to the other between the Christian discerners and the Navy. They wanted to move on, but so-called proof from both sides unnerved them.

While the families continued to boil in the caldron of confusion, Marilyn moved on to untangle surprises and mysteries. Even after the crash site was located, her work had just begun. From out of her research of every lead, she prepared a significant body of evidence that indicated the Department of Defense may have known the location of the missing plane within the first week, possibly within two days [Appendix 1].

"I'd rather credit God with the miracle of helping us locate the plane than believe that my fellow human beings would deceive me," Marilyn said. And she would rather believe that malfunction caused their descent and crash than the preposterous claim of pilot error.

Contradictions within investigative reports from General Electric, which makes the engine, from McDonnell-Douglas, which manufactures the plane, and opinions from Navy officials intruded continually on any possibility of closure [Appendix 2]. As a result, Marilyn collected and organized twelve pages of documented data to support the theory that the F-18 crashed as the result of malfunction rather than pilot error [Appendix 3]. Explaining her theories to the commander who refuted them, Marilyn questioned his assertions.

"That scenario doesn't make sense to me."

"It doesn't have to make sense to you. That's just the way it is," he responded curtly. Marilyn's tenacity and courage in the face of humiliation and stonewalling is a remarkable tribute to her. Impatience and frustration on both sides triggered questions and often revealed answers that neither the Navy nor the families wanted to accept.

Her attorneys received copies of both Marilyn's and the military's investigative reports, as did United States Senators Don Nickles, Strom Thurmond, Alfonse D'Amato, John McCain, Sam Nunn and Alan Dixon, from whom she requested aid. In turn, they requested complete copies of the initial (1987) and revised (1988) JAG and Mishap reports; written answers from the Department of Defense to Marilyn's list of written questions; reasons for withholding information from the families, the general public, and especially the search pilots about the actual last known position of the aircraft; reasons for either concealing the report of a crash in the Green Creek Canyon area or refusal to act on the information; flight reports of the search aircraft from the Army Aviation Support Facility in Reno, Nevada; information about "classified material" at Scott Aerospace Rescue and Recovery Center, the Pentagon and the Naval Safety Center in Norfolk, Virginia.

Responding to Senator Don Nickles' request for information, the Rear Admiral Commander of the Light Attack Wing of the Pacific Fleet steered the discourse in his letter to one conclusion: *pilot error* [Appendix 4]. Obviously, these two words summarized the position of the Navy. Not only the families, but also numerous officials, pilots, Attorney Brown and others questioned that assumption.

Interviewed by Bill O'Reilly for *Inside Edition*, Marilyn appeared on nationwide telecasts in April, 1988. Her story also appeared in Jack Anderson's syndicated column published in scores of newspapers [Appendix 5]. In it the writer stated, "The Pentagon has locked the records of the crash in a vault for top-secret material and will release only a sanitized version of its conclusions." He also suggested "the Navy should thank Mrs. Ginsberg. Until she found the F-18, it was the only military jet lost inside the United States in the past 10 years."

So, major syndicated columnists did not have any more luck getting answers than the rest of us. Intentionally mute even about unclassified information, the Navy repeatedly denied access to investigative documents requested by the families within the Freedom of Information Act. In the sanitized reports that the families received from the military, with obliterated paragraphs and omitted pages, someone had scribbled in those "silent" spaces: *None of your business.* Whose business was it, then?

On June 9, 1989, more than two years following the mishap and one year after the plane was found, the commander again shocked the families when he wrote a numbered review of the facts, but omitted numbers 3-22 and the final page(s) in the *unclassified* document. The concluding statement in the Analysis of Findings declared that the examination of all maintenance records revealed "no existing engine, flight control, hydraulic, electrical, aircraft balance, or other discrepancies that would affect its capability to perform the assigned mission." Yet, all information preceding the summary was deleted. What was missing?

A Navy official on behalf of the Naval Safety Center in Norfolk, Virginia, explained the reasons for withholding the unclassified information requested by the families. After nearly three years of requesting information, the reply was the same:

> "Enclosed is a redacted copy of the original and supplemental Mishap Investigation Report (MIR) including those portions containing factual information and withholding subjective evaluations, opinions, speculation and privileged statements of witnesses given with the promise of confidentiality.
>
> "The government has a legitimate interest in withholding those portions of the report containing subjective evaluations because these investigations are conducted solely to prevent the loss of life and property. The limitation we impose on the release of these personal opinions and speculations encourages an open, frank and honest discussion of the events surrounding mishaps leading, in turn, to safer operations for Navy and Marine personnel worldwide."

Of course, the reasons for this are not all bad. Both witnesses and manufacturers such as McDonnell-Douglas, General Dynamics and General Electric, by being provided immunity, can be straightforward in their disclosures. These may be valid reasons for the "none of your business" attitude. The problem is, according to the mother of James Victoria who was also killed in an accident, the military and the manufacturers "investigate themselves. They're their own judge and jury" [Appendix 6]. Attorney Richard Brown in San Francisco agrees.

While some professionals argue that cover-up is in the best interest of both safety and the design and manufacture of planes and equipment, others disagree. Accepting responsibility and welcoming independent investigations may improve rather than diminish safety for military pilots.

Don and Naomi sent a letter to Navy officials to express their loyalty and respect for the military. They added, "We want to know the truth . . . that is all. Is that asking too much?"

Yet, they continued to accept *not knowing*, the lack of answers, as God's way of saying: *Wait*. "Since the Lord is directing our steps," an ancient wise man asked, "why try to understand everything that happens along the way" (Proverbs 20:24)?

When had it become *us* versus *them*? Every so-called answer prompted new questions. Theological, philosophical, technical, rhetorical, the questions accumulated from every direction, every source. Having lived through this bizarre story, Marilyn knows much of what she documented may have no bearing on what actually happened. "But somewhere in this collection," she said, "is the truth."

"This last year has been a living hell," Marilyn continued. "I have gone from grieving to blaming Dan for his own death, from questioning my sanity to being convinced I am on the right track." With accumulating evidence pointing toward malfunction of Raider 58, she began to direct anger at herself for having doubted Dan's abilities as a pilot. She had traveled the arduous and risky route that gradually led her from blindly trusting the Navy to doubting everything any military or government official said to her.

But, she didn't want it to be that way. Neither did the Navy.

* * * * *

By that time the number of people who believed Mike was alive had dwindled to practically none, other than the clairvoyants back in Bartlesville. After pieces of the aircraft but still no body remains were located, the families stood poised, actually ready in a detached sort of way, for the news they wanted to hear.

Finally, the call came: "We've recovered some bones." It splashed over their consciousness more like a ripple than the initial tidal wave that broke over them more than a year earlier. Of course, the families pictured "some bones." What they got were bone fragments that introduced another long saga.

I had wondered what Connie and Betty would do with information about bones, but they did with it what they'd been doing. Finding bones meant nothing until the pathologist identified them. That should take no longer than a few days.

If the cause of the mishap was not the "business" of the families, surely identification of the body fragments was their business. On July 5, Marilyn learned the team had extracted a piece of t-shirt material and a piece of velcro from a flight suit with hair adhering to both. Sounding urgent, an official requested a sample of Dan's hair, as from a hairbrush, for a comparative analysis. He also asked Marilyn to ask Dan's parents about giving blood samples. CDR Torrence picked up the hair samples. However, the results of the hair analysis have yet to be given to Marilyn, and the Ginsbergs were never contacted regarding blood samples. All remains were forwarded to the Armed Forces Institute of Pathology (AFIP) in Washington, D.C., for DNA "fingerprinting." In 1988, the process was still in its infancy. As every cell is unique, identification is 99.999 percent accurate and usually results in conclusive answers. A few more weeks would not matter.

Then came the extraordinary saga of finding one of Mike's teeth on the mountain, identified as Mike's by comparing it with an x-ray. Mike only had one filling, and it so happened that was the tooth found on Kavanaugh Ridge. Truly miraculous, like the folded parachutes it was conclusive evidence that Mike was killed in the crash. No doubts lingered—but only for a short time. A Navy official later informed the family it was not confirmed to be a human tooth. With a filling? Or, did it not have a filling?

"We want to accept what they tell us," Naomi said, "but the information seems so confusing." It was confusing. The pendulum ticked on.

Finally, the families decided to forego positive identification. Having accepted that the tooth was Mike's and the bone fragments were the remains of Mike and Dan, they began to plan the service at Arlington National Cemetery. But by that time the Navy had decided to continue its attempts to identify the remains definitively.

At last the AFIP called. Of 21 pieces of remains, they had positively identified at least one piece for each man. Marilyn pictured her husband's body as she liked to remember it. But, she really wanted to know one more thing. "What body parts have been identified as Dan's?" she quietly asked the officer. She wondered how she could be asking such a question about her beloved husband.

"Why do you always ask such insignificant questions?" he bristled.

Jarred from her reverie, Marilyn hurtled back at him, "If these were your wife's remains we were talking about, the questions would not seem insignificant. Please get back to me with the answer."

She inquired how long it would take to identify the rest of the remains. He said that at that rate, it would probably be a few more months, as one piece was identified in early August, four by early September, and six as of late September. Puzzled, Marilyn asked why she had not been notified until then, if some remains had been identified two months earlier. "Also, if the procedure takes so long, why not process all 21 pieces simultaneously? Why do one at a time?"

As the families needed only one positive ID for individual graves at Arlington National Cemetery, they returned to planning the service. Naomi had told her daughters they would have only one service at Arlington if the remains were not identified, but that if any pieces were positively identified, she and Don wanted a graveside service also in Bartlesville. With Lenore and other family members, Nadean struggled like an insect caught in a web, hopelessly jerked one way and then another, trying to escape the confusion that surrounded her.

"We've already had two—one in California the first week, and then the memorial service in Bartlesville on their wedding weekend," Nadean exploded to her parents uncharacteristically. "Now, we're talking about another one in Arlington, and then a funeral back home? No! I can't take any more."

Then CDR Torrence reported that the pathologists at AFIP had just come up with a new process. They would definitely be able to have the rest of the remains identified within one to two weeks. That was good news; the families could certainly wait a few more weeks. But in late October, he said the new process had not worked. It could be months before the rest of the remains could be identified. Marilyn told him she would consult with family members before making the decision—again. And again, they decided to wait it out.

"The whole situation was bizarre," Marilyn said. If paleontologists can identify bones thousands of years old, why was this particular task so difficult and time-consuming? The MIA remains returned to the United States from Vietnam in the summer of 1988 had already been identified. Surely those remains were more deteriorated than those of Dan and Mike, and the pathologists conducting the ID process probably had no clue as to their actual identity. Why then, after having the remains under scrutiny for a longer period of time, and having to differentiate between only two men, had they been unable to identify them?

Finally, the Muellers called Marilyn with this news: The identification process was complete. Dr. Dawson, the pathologist from the AFIP, said they had positively identified five pieces of soft tissue as Dan's, and two pieces as Mike's based on blood types. The DNA processing had not been successful, and they could not ID the rest of the remains for various reasons. However, other research labs could attempt other techniques on the remains if they chose to continue.

The families were ready for closure, just short of two years since the men disappeared. Marilyn called Dr. Dawson. "We want to make an informed decision and proceed with burial," she explained wearily. "Will you please send a report of the findings in writing?"

"No way," he said.

Maybe that was none of the families' business, either. In fact, it was not until six years after the mishap—six years of unresponsiveness—that the AFIP forwarded the first pathology report to the Muellers, indicating the lone tooth had indeed been identified as Mike's [Appendix 7]. None of their business, indeed.

The night before the families met friends at Arlington National Cemetery, they gathered to view the remains. Arranged on satin, a handful of thimble-sized wax containers encased tiny bone fragments, the bodily remains of two giants among men.

Don and Naomi noted the time. Exactly two years earlier at that very hour, two Marine officers had parked their vehicle and walked up to the stone house on Polaris Drive in Bartlesville with life-changing news. Of course, they could not see their loved one laid out for a last viewing. Instead, each embraced a precious memory. They opened a new channel into which their eternal spring of hope flowed.

Clearly, there was more beyond a Mishap Investigative Report and a JAG Manual, more than a bone and a tooth, more beyond Kavanaugh Ridge and even Arlington National Cemetery . . .

CHAPTER 16

NEW DIMENSION

When you soared on silver wings, we envied you.
Now that your soul has taken wings to be with your God,
we envy you still . . .
We miss you, Flyboy! But we will not say good-bye.
We will grieve, long and hard,
but we will grieve with joy . . .
—Rick Griffin, 1987

Along the winding road through Arlington National Cemetery, I walked with family and friends behind a horse-drawn caisson bearing two caskets with a handful of fragments in each. Brought together in a profoundly symbolic way, Mike and Dan were no longer First Lieutenant and Captain, Wesleyan and Episcopalian, Oklahoman and New Yorker. As United States Marines who had flown F-18's for the Navy, their physical mortality had become their commonality.

Duplicating thousands of others on the rolling hillsides in Arlington, Virginia, the rituals and sounds seeped through our senses into our souls. The Marine band played. Spontaneous laughter and friendly smiles invited us to live again. God's presence warmed the cold of finality. A black-capped chickadee watched from a grave marker. Exquisitely dressed trees bowed low toward a long line of mourners. They had watched the scene often. They would watch it again.

Sitting with family and friends, I clung to the reading of these ancient words from Ecclesiastes: "For everything its season, and for every activity under heaven its time: A time to be born and a time to die . . ." When Mike left for flight school, I gave him a scroll inscribed with those words. Thinking it was for him, I never imagined its wisdom was also for me. The minister added to the litany: " . . . a time to hold on and a time to let go." It was time to commit my unanswered questions, my grief—and Mike—to God.

The minister reminded those gathered that Mike could never be contained in a box, or reduced to ashes. A powerful life cannot be snuffed out. But I was still learning what that meant.

The abrupt report of the sixteen-gun salute shattered the silence. It echoed around and around through the rolling hillsides dotted with monuments and crosses—and shot through me. Inside, my composure cracked. I winced. I wanted to cap my ears and hide, but instead stood motionless. The sound embodied the precipitous intervention of tragedy, the shattered dreams, the evaporation of the blessed ordinariness of life. Repeated hundreds of times every year, this time it was for me. I had lost not only Mike, but part of myself. Or so I thought then.

* * * * *

It was two years later. I pulled to the edge of the winding road where I had followed family and friends behind the horse-drawn caisson on May 21, 1989. Beneath a dusky green sassafras tree I found Mike's grave. Years earlier I had stooped to pluck another dusky green plant that had pushed upward through a crack in the granite of Kavanaugh Ridge. There, crushing the sagebrush between my fingers, I had wrestled with the monstrous realization that death was the last enemy one day to be destroyed. I had tightened my fist around the finality, the meaninglessness, the utter stupidity of Mike's apparent end on the ridge. Even believing he was with God had not concluded my search.

But finally, I could stop looking. I had found Mike, though not as expected. Life had not ended on Kavanaugh Ridge; it had not ended two years later in Arlington National Cemetery. A stone marked the resting place for the agony of the waiting game that lasted two years. I had buried there the excruciating pain, but had not left Mike where white crosses stand erect in straight rows as far as the eye can see.

Through the years I had gradually discovered the secret, one encounter at a time. It began with Mike's presence with me in the kitchen the morning after he disappeared. He was so tangibly real that I whirled around to embrace him. Though his body was not there—his spirit was. A presence. A living, spirit presence. That's why Mick still asks his advice, and why Ron still talks to him when flying.

There was more. Mike's likeness in a stranger had more than once startled me. His spirit-image imprinted in his friends astounded me. Even his namesakes added a "new dimension to fill the void," as Gene said about his baby Michael. Finally, it all added up. The ultimate flight transported Mike not only into the presence of God, but also into "an added new dimension," a part of the mystery of death.

We are more than human beings. We are spiritual beings, and the spirit does not die. Mike is spirit. He yet lives within and around us. Those welcome and unexpected vivid encounters—in strangers, in Mike's friends, in his presence—remind me that the powerful spirit-life lives on. He has joined that "great cloud of witnesses" who cheer us on in our journeys.

Warm sun filtered through the sassafras tree. Stretching upward, I broke off a tiny twig. I traced its three distinctive leaves, each a different shape, all on one tree. Suddenly it symbolized for me the three dimensions of Mike's life: his physical presence while he lived with us; his ongoing presence in spirit; his eternal life in God's presence. The anonymous voice that could be Mike's spoke:

Do not stand at my grave and weep;
I am not there. I do not sleep . . .
Do not stand at my grave and cry;
I am not there. I did not die.

One day we will talk about this, Mike. But for now, I accept your presence as God's gift.

EPILOGUE: LIFE GOES ON

Mike's vision for missions and ministry lives on through financial and time commitments given by friends and family as a monument to Mike's life. They include Lumley Wesleyan Church built in Sierra Leone, Africa; mission projects in Israel, Brazil, Thailand, Japan, Vietnam and Mexico; the Mike Mueller Memorial Youth Center built at First Wesleyan Church in Bartlesville, Oklahoma; the American Bible Society and the Gideons; a lighting system in Hanford (California) Church of the Nazarene, where Mike attended on his last Sunday.

Mike's parents have accepted their son's death as part of God's plan "from the beginning of Mike's life, and even from the beginning of time." Typical of their faith, Don says, "We try to see it all from God's perspective." They are thankful for increased empathy toward others who are suffering, and that their loss has neither embittered them nor introduced a wedge between them. Mike would have relished his new role as brother-in-law to Darrell Eash and Jeff Charonnat and as uncle to his sisters' children, Andrew Michael and Natalie Anne.

Lenore, too, lives on. During the winter of 1991 when U.S. troops went to defend Kuwait, she often felt Mike's presence. Hearing the first pilot casualty was named Mike and flying an F-18, Lenore wept. "I'm so glad you're not there," she told him. Happily married to a "most wonderful" Pete Swanson, she is the mother of Karl and Kristen. Healing continues. "Joy and peace through Christ Jesus" fill her life.

For Mike's friends, as well, life goes on. Alan Chamberlain continues to enjoy his "new life" in Christ. Gene Snyman, now an army captain serving in Bosnia, continues to experience God at work as a result of Mike's influence.

Marilyn, having packed all her research into boxes to store in the attic, wrote, "I will not open that box again, but perhaps my children may want to see it some day. All along, I felt God leading me. Then, one day God told me that journey was over. God still leads me, but in a different direction now." Happy with her new husband and baby daughter, Marilyn teaches Sunday School and her children about Jesus. "As always," she says, "I'm on my own journey to know God better, too . . ."

"I have no intention of writing anything at all about this [part of my life]," Marilyn told me. "Martha, follow the Spirit within you . . ."

That I have done.

CONTENTS FOR APPENDICES

APPENDIX 1

In support of the theory that the DOD knew the location within first week.

Shocking evidence in the JAG report suggested that Scott ARRC and the DOD knew the correct coordinates of the last known position (LKP) within two days. However, during the first month, DOD officials told the families the LKP was north of Glass Mountain and that the area was being searched repeatedly using maps with radar coordinates leading to that area.

The families learned of the amended LKP in June 1987 from a civilian source. Neither the XO nor the squadron pilots who had participated in dozens of sorties during official searches had been informed of the revised LKP; likewise, neither the Mono County Sheriffs Department nor the staff at the U.S. Forest Service (that owns the property) had been informed that the plane disappeared from radar within their jurisdiction.

Major Rushmore of the Nevada Wing of the CAP, highly experienced in searching for missing aircraft, stated that more than 90 percent of downed aircraft are found within 2-3 miles from the point at which they disappear from radar. But the NWCAP was specifically told not to fly south of Bridgeport during the initial 2-3 days of their participation in the search. The actual crash site turned out to be less than three miles south of the LKP.

A year later when Marilyn prepared the master map to publicize her own search, CDR Whitten, an experienced pilot who knows how to read and print radar plots, encouraged her to highlight the area *north* of the LKP on the master map. After hundreds of maps had been mailed, Marilyn discovered that the radar plots Whitten had printed were incorrect and misleading. Based then on her own research, the widow's volunteers found the plane within seven hours.

In response to the families' request for a list of all leads, including crank phone calls and psychic predictions, the Navy never alluded to a report of crash sounds in Green Creek Drainage Area. When Marilyn discovered and reported that information a year later, it was shrugged off as "an old lead." By its own admission, the Navy had been aware of that report just after the plane disappeared. Therefore, 1) the Navy was aware of the location and did not follow through, or 2) it searched the area and did not find what the widow found more than a year later, or

3) it located the missing plane the first couple of days and proceeded with a cover-up.

Omitted from the JAG report were satellite weather maps closest to the mishap time. Instead, maps for late morning—as the weather changed—were produced as "evidence" of weather factors. Also, in the days following the disappearance, the families were told there were no radar tapes. They believed that until the briefing at Lemoore in April 1988, during which the families were given written material that summarized the information. It included this: *Radar tapes from Oakland Center, China Lake and Fallon were reviewed.* How could that information have been accurate if the Navy had no tapes?

Marilyn hired a private investigator who went to the Oakland Air Traffic Control (ATC) and to the Federal Aviation Administration (FAA) in San Francisco. He learned that all the records regarding the mishap had been forwarded to the safety officer at VFA-125. Is that standard procedure? It appears highly unlikely that no records are retained at Oakland ATC, the civilian monitoring facility.

Furthermore, eyewitness accounts by two civilians and a deputy sheriff testified to sighting a sky crane and two UH-1 helicopters flying into Green Creek Drainage Area along the Kavanaugh Ridge, on the afternoon of the mishap and days immediately following. A sky crane is not a search aircraft; it is extremely expensive to operate; it's use is relegated to specific capabilities: to lift or lower cargo, especially into or out of areas that are not easily accessible.

Yet, the 1987 JAG report specifically states that the search aircraft on the day of the mishap did not fly south of Bridgeport, making the witness statements and the JAG report directly contradictory. The Army Aviation Support Facility (AASF) in Reno, Nevada, did send aircraft to Fallon NAS on four days of the initial ten-day search and did not deny having flown sky crane(s) into Green Creek Canyon. When asked why a sky crane was used, they suggested they wanted to be as much help as possible, so utilized any available aircraft.

The DOD had both the capability and motivation to find the F-18, yet many of the resources were not utilized. To assist Marilyn, Major Rushmore (NWCAP) requested grids for previous searches to avoid duplication, but the files were classified and therefore, unavailable. The JAG report and MIR had an unknown number of pages missing, such as pages 2-10 of the MIR and numerous white spaces in which material had been deleted. What could be "classified" in so-called "unclassified" documents about a search for a missing airplane?

LT Jordan, the pilot-in-command in the F-18 that was flying about ten minutes behind the mishap plane, stated he last saw on radar what he believed to be the mishap aircraft, northeast of Mono Lake. Jordan's statement fits the false radar report which put the plane in front of Glass Mountain. But, it is now known that the mishap plane never made it to the area northeast of Mono Lake. The radar data from Oakland ATC indicated that there were no other aircraft in the vicinity at the time of the mishap. On what did LT Jordan base his statement?

The Navy omitted from the JAG report the witness statement of the front-seat pilot with Jordan. LT Bernard, who last communicated with Mike and Dan, contradicted LT Jordan's testimony, stating he last saw the mishap aircraft 1-2 minutes prior to the plane's disappearance in the vicinity of the true LKP. The Navy insisted that the pilots' last radio contact was at least five minutes after the plane disappeared from radar. Yet Bernard's statement was omitted from the JAG report. The Navy had it, but hid it. Did they act on it? Did they locate the plane?

Based on interviews of squadron pilots nearly two weeks following the mishap, the misquotations, inaccuracies and contradictions concerning times and locations in both the witness statements and the endorsements in the JAG report can be understood—though not excused—as conjecture after a two-week hiatus. Witnesses ordinarily are interviewed immediately. Audio recordings of time of day and communications among the pilots during flight were not available.

Several enclosures included in the 1987 JAG report "have not been certified as true copies." This convenience protects all except the fall guy, the victim, the scapegoat, the one responsible for the mishap blamed on "pilot error."

APPENDIX 2

Some Contradictions and Questions

Appendix 1 describes the contradictions between two witness statements. Not only were the pilots not interviewed for two weeks, but also, the contradictory testimony of the pilot who *accurately identified the LKP* was omitted. In addition to this and others suggested in Appendix 1, further discrepancies appeared within the General Electric (GE) report, the military Mishap Investigative Report (MIR) and summation letters with opinions by Navy personnel.

While the summary statement in the GE report declared that the *"standby airspeed indicator could not determine aircraft airspeed at impact,"* a statement in the same document indicated that *" . . . the standby airspeed indicator revealed aircraft airspeed at impact to be 350-400 knots."*

Reports concerning the condition of motor components indicated that *"both engines were operating at approximately 84-89 percent core speed,"* suggesting no evidence of *"any major failure of engine turbomachinery."* Yet, according to the auditory witnesses (Attorney Richard Brown and his daughter) camping within two miles of the crash site, *no sound* was audible even though the plane had to have passed almost directly overhead at low altitude moments before it crashed.

From out of nine key findings a point of confusion arose regarding this statement: *Neither fan exhibited classical evidence of high speed rotor rotation.* The examiner theorized that either rotor rotation stopped suddenly at ground impact, or the casing tore away from the rotor rather than being crushed into it at ground impact. If, however, *neither fan exhibited classical evidence of high speed rotor rotation,* why not as quickly assume the rotor was not moving *before* impact?

Another report suggested that the F404 engine in the F-18 ordinarily remains intact when crashed, but that *"as a result of this crash into solid rock,"* both engines were broken into small pieces, *"making definitive evaluation demanding."* The examiner also stated that both high speed and high angle of impact do the work of breaking up engines, but he concluded that in this instance, the small pieces indicated that the engines were running. Would not, as first stated, a high-speed impact into solid rock result in breaking the engines into small pieces, whether or not the engines were functioning?

The investigation provided information in spite of often ambiguous, evasive or contradictory conclusions. For example, Navy personnel [quote] *found the six bombs the plane was carrying.* Officials at

Lemoore had helped Marilyn prepare the poster included in the packet mailed out to publicize her private search. She would not have known whether the F-18 carried bombs; it was officials who added *the jet carried no ordnance*. Why had the military added that false statement? Or, did it not carry six bombs?

Both angle and direction of impact affects the distribution and recovery of body parts. Having been led to believe the plane had crashed head-on, the families were surprised when CDR Torrence responded to later questioning: "No, the plane did not go in nose first, if that's what you're asking. The rear of the plane was the first part to impact the ridge." They later read what one examiner wrote: *"The attitude of the plane at the time of impact cannot be determined."* Yet still another investigator reported it impacted in a *"level attitude on a heading of 120 degrees."*

Another area of contradictions exists in reports of the AFIP concerning examination of body remains. The remains from site A were assumed to be Mike's. The entry for A-21 stated: "A-21 tooth with amalgam filling." A lab report dated July 1988 added: "This specimen is an intact tooth with stringy and fibrous attachments at the root. Some enamel is chipped off the surface due to either normal occlusal trauma or impact trauma. The apical third of the mesio-facial root is fractured off. The tooth is properly identified as the maxillary right first molar (#3) or possibly the second molar. It has an old lingual pit amalgam restoration. Upon comparison with copies of the dental records of the two presumed deceased servicemembers, the tooth unquestionably is #3 and belongs to First Lieutenant Michael D. Mueller 509 54 5804 USMC."

I later questioned the AFIP about information given to families that the tooth was subsequently regarded as possibly "not of human origin." The written response from the Office of Legal Counsel stated: "With respect to a report on a tooth, neither AFIP records nor [the pathologist] is aware of a tooth report." Of course, this was later corrected when the Muellers received their *first* written pathology report in 1993.

In yet another report, specimen A-21 is described—not as a tooth—but as "a bone fragment measuring 2 1/2 x 3/4 x 3/8 inches. One surface is white, while the other surface consists of a marrow cavity with almost no trabecular bone remaining. There is an indentation along one edge of the specimen due to focal crushing, with connecting slightly displaced fractures extending away from, but not completely across, the fragment . . . This bone fragment is very dried compared with the moistness of the other specimens. There is a tiny amount of soft tissue near one end . . ."

APPENDIX 3

Possible Causes of the Mishap

At the time of the mishap, the recurrent problem of engine fires, as well as other problems in the F-18, was not public knowledge. [See article following.] Once the recurrent problems became apparent, the DOD issued specific directives to prevent emergencies from occurring and designed emergency/corrective procedures as well. Dan and Mike, of course, did not have the benefit of knowing these special procedures. Both engines of the mishap plane were in excess of the recommended 800 flight hours with 1,482.9 hours for the port engine and 955.4 for the starboard engine. Had it survived, it would have been grounded with the others. Accounts from surviving F-18 pilots concerning the other F-18 crashes include engine fires that could not be extinguished and inability to control the planes.

Examiners do not believe that the many outstanding maintenance technical directives for Raider 58 had any bearing on the crash. The aircraft's sudden swerve to the left prior to disappearing from radar headed the plane southwest. But the last radio communication, just one to two minutes prior to this turn, indicated they would head east or northeast, making it appear that this sudden turn to the southwest was not an intentional change in direction. The aircraft also slowed down prior to disappearing from radar, and then suddenly disappeared while at an altitude of 18,500 feet, well above any mountainous terrain in the area.

The crash site was located within three miles from where the plane disappeared, headed in the same direction as it last appeared on radar. This is consistent with the studied opinion of aerodynamic physicists who claim the plane probably would have gone that distance had it continued to decelerate at the same rate/direction before crashing. Furthermore, the crash site was within two miles of the auditory witness. Based on the crash site and the direction the plane was headed when it crashed, it would have passed almost directly overhead of the witness in the quiet of the Hoover Wilderness area. Had the engines been running, the witness would have heard the sound prior to impact, as the F-18 engines function at extremely high decibels, even at idle.

Some officials acknowledged that the plane began to descend at the point it disappeared from radar, but reasoned that "pilot error" caused the descent. The commander theorized that the engines were functioning "100 percent properly; [the pilots] turned off the IFF transponder, descended, and covered 360 degrees which brought them back to the LKP, but at a much lower altitude . . . they headed south again and impacted into Kavanaugh for an unknown reason."

The IFF transponder on fighter planes enhances radar images. While some Navy officials vehemently maintained the pilots turned off their IFF transponder, allowing them to have flown without being tracked, some pilots and other experts argued that even if deactivated, radar could have tracked the weaker signal. The primary reason a plane disappears totally from radar is flying low-level. Many believe that is exactly the reason Raider 58 disappeared without warning: It rapidly descended.

So, why did the plane descend precipitously? Marilyn theorized three possible explanations: First, *intentional descent*. The pilots were aware that the highest peak in this quadrant is 12,800 feet. They know to fly no lower than 3 thousand feet *above* this point. Barring suicide, there is no way they would have descended intentionally to 10,400 feet, far below any safety parameters.

Even if they intentionally descended, the auditory witness indicated the ridge was not snow-covered or obscured prior to the mishap. Camping within two miles of the crash site that morning, Brown stated the weather was clear with some high cirrus clouds, and the mountain was not obscured. Although the weather did deteriorate later that day, it was at the very least fair in the immediate area of the mishap at that hour of the morning. It is highly unlikely that weather was a factor in this incident. Brown should know. He photographed Kavanaugh Ridge soon after hearing the impact. The clear, crisp image of the mountain is now in possession of Mike's parents. Of course, the Navy neither interviewed the witness nor saw the photograph.

Next, Marilyn examined the possibility of *unintentional descent caused by pilot error*. For this to have occurred, it is assumed one or both pilots made a serious mistake, causing the plane to descend; that neither pilot was able to correct that mistake; and finally, that neither of the pilots recognized the potentially fatal situation and therefore failed to initiate the ejection procedure. That's too many assumptions for any who know these two men to accept.

The third possibility was *unintentional descent caused by malfunction*. If this occurred, it is unlikely the plane could respond to manual input for emergency procedures, resulting in a spin or dive that would preempt ejection. To many, this scenario has the most validity. I shudder to think the men may have recognized an emergency that surpassed their ability to respond.

From *The Washington Post*, November 21, 1987, A8:

Engine Problems Ground 250 Fighter Jets

By Molly Moore
Washington Post Staff Writer

The Navy and Marine Corps have ordered about 250 of their FA18 Hornet fighter jets grounded because of potential engine fires that were blamed for three crashes and suspected as the cause of a fourth crash on Monday, according to Pentagon officials.

"The flight restriction is necessary to reduce the risk of further aircraft loss due to uncontained titanium fires" in the engines, the Navy said.

The Navy has been investigating problems with the General Electric F404 engines after crashes were caused when blades in the engines' high pressure compressor broke, causing internal fires that burned through the engine casings and into flight control and other nearby systems, Navy officials said.

A West Coast Navy official said the decision, announced yesterday, to ground about 250 of the 384 Hornets in active service came after the crash Monday of a Marine Hornet in California. Although the cause of that crash has not been officially determined, it is believed to have been caused by the same type of engine problems that led to three previous crashes, the official said.

Navy officials said no pilots have been killed in any of the crashes.

The Hornet is a twin-engine tactical aircraft used by the Navy and Marine Corps as fighter escorts and for air defense of naval fleets. The planes, which cost about $32.7 million each, also can be used as strike fighters.

A California Navy official involved in the Hornet program said the grounding of the planes involves most of the aircraft assigned to the carrier USS Coral Sea in the Mediterranean and a few craft assigned to the carrier USS Midway in the Northern Arabian Sea.

"If operational necessity dictates, FA18s are fully capable of responding to any threat," the Navy said in a prepared statement.

The "flight restrictions" were issued for all engines with more than 800 hours flight time, the Navy said. Navy officials said they believe that from one-third to one-half of the 1,000 operational and spare F404 engines would be affected.

Navy officials said the flawed parts of the engines are being redesigned and tested. Officials said it has not yet been determined whether the Navy or General Electric will absorb the cost of the redesign and the repairs.

Both the blades and the casings in the engine are made of titanium, officials said. "When they [the blades] come apart, they fly like missiles," one official said.

Canada recently refused to accept delivery of an order of the fighters from McDonnell Douglas because of the same problems in the General Electric engines after the crash of a Canadian plane.

Reprint of article from *Washington Post*, November 21, 1987, A8 as seen above:

Engine Problems Ground 250 Fighter Jets
By Molly Moore, Washington Post Staff Writer

The Navy and Marine Corps have ordered about 250 of their FA18 Hornet fighter jets grounded because of potential engine fires that were blamed for three crashes and suspected as the cause of a fourth crash on Monday, according to Pentagon officials.

"The flight restriction is necessary to reduce the risk of further aircraft loss due to uncontained titanium fires in the engines," the Navy said.

The Navy has been investigating problems with the General Electric F404 engines after crashes were caused when blades in the engines' high pressure compressor broke, causing internal fires that burned through the engine casings and into flight control and other nearby systems, Navy officials said.

A West Coast Navy official said the decision, announced yesterday, to ground about 250 of the 384 Hornets in active service came after the crash Monday of a Marine Hornet in California. Although the cause of the crash has not been officially determined, it is believed to have been caused by the same type of engine problems that led to three previous crashes, the official said.

Navy officials said no pilots have been killed in any of the crashes.

The Hornet is a twin-engine tactical aircraft used by the Navy and Marine Corps as fighter escorts and for air defense of naval fleets. The planes, which cost about $32.7 million each, also can be used as strike fighters.

A California Navy official involved in the Hornet program said the grounding of the planes involves most of the aircraft assigned to the carrier Coral Sea in the Mediterranean and a few craft assigned to the carrier USS Midway in the Northern Arabian Sea.

"If operational necessity dictates, FA18s are fully capable of responding to any threat," the Navy said in a prepared statement.

The "flight restrictions" were issued for all engines with more than 800 hours flight time, the Navy said. Navy officials said they believe that from one-third to one-half of the 1,000 operational and spare F404 engines would be affected.

Navy officials said the flawed parts of the engines are being redesigned and tested. Officials said it has not yet been determined whether the Navy and General Electric will absorb the cost of the redesign and the repairs.

Both the blades and the casings in the engine are made of titanium, officials said. "When they [the blades] come apart, they fly like missiles," one official said.

Canada recently refused to accept delivery of an order of the fighters from McDonnell-Douglas because of the same problems in the General Electric engines after the crash of a Canadian plane.

APPENDIX 4

Letter from Rear Admiral Commander of the Pacific Fleet

In response to a letter from Senator Don Nickles (Oklahoma) who questioned the assumed cause as pilot error, the commander wrote:

". . . you raise a question with regard to that portion of my letter to you dated January 18, 1990, in which I explained why the focus of the Navy's search for the mishap site was 30 miles south of where the mishap aircraft was last recorded on radar by the Oakland Air Route Traffic Control Center. My explanation noted that Raider 58 stopped emitting [the transponder] signal at an altitude just above 18,000 feet at 0903 on the morning of the mishap.

"In your letter, you state 'neither [Captain Ginsberg nor First Lieutenant Mueller] had ever been known to break flight rules such as turning off a transponder or violating the 18,000 MSL altitude rule.' I cannot respond to that assertion. The Manual of the Judge Advocate General (JAG) Investigation into the mishap did not attempt to ascertain whether either Captain Ginsberg or First Lieutenant Mueller had ever broken an altitude restriction . . .

"You continue in paragraph 3 stating that 'there is no substantiated evidence to suggest that either pilot would have done this before the fatal crash.' I direct your attention to enclosure (4) of the JAG Manual Investigation. That enclosure reflects that between 0903:06 and 0903:18, Raider 58 entered restricted airspace above 18,000 feet MSL. At 0903:06, Raider 58 was at 18,500 feet MSL. At 0903:30, Raider 58 was still at 18,500 feet MSL. It was at that time that Raider 58's transponder stopped transmitting.

"As I stated in my letter of January 18, 1990, radio transmissions from Raider 58 were received by other aircraft belonging to Strike Fighter Squadron 125 as late as 0922 on the morning of the mishap. None of those radio transmissions from Raider 58 contained any information which would lead one to conclude that Raider 58 was experiencing any mechanical or electronic malfunction during that 18-19 minute period.

"In light of that fact, the only logical conclusion that can be reached is that Raider 58 was not experiencing any mechanical or electronic malfunction which degraded its ability to communicate or to be flown. In view of the fact that Raider 58's transponder stopped transmitting while the aircraft was in restricted airspace without the required clearance and Raider 58 was flown without apparent difficulty for 18-19 minutes thereafter, based on my experience I consider it a valid conclusion that the mishap pilots purposely deactivated the transponder in Raider 58. As I stated in my previous letter, aircrews have been known to deactivate their transponders when deviating from their specific air space clearances in an attempt to avoid the entry of flight violations in their records. Accordingly, the assumption concerning the deactivation of Raider 58's transponder made by those directing the search effort were appropriate at the time; and they remain appropriate today.

"You asked whether the mishap involving Captain Ginsberg and First Lieutenant Mueller could be 'classified as pilot error beyond a reasonable doubt.' In attempting to determine the cause of a mishap which occurs under circumstances similar to this, there will always be unanswered questions. I note, however, that all known facts point to the conclusion that pilot error was the cause of this mishap. Those factors are as follows [brackets/italics mine]:

a. Raider 58's flight path was approximately level at the time of impact.
[*See contradictions in Appendix 2. Attitude not known.*]

b. Both engines were operating properly and at normal speed at time of impact.
[*The engine "was broken in small pieces." Refer to Appendix 2.*]

c. No pre-mishap engine malfunction could be discovered.
[*Not only were the engines broken in small pieces, but also, no engine sound was heard overhead by the witness moments before the crash. The expert witness camping in the area, an attorney who investigates air crashes, was not questioned. See Appendix 3.*]

d. Neither mishap pilot had initiated the ejection sequence at the time of impact.
[*What bearing does this have on the pilots' culpability? If they realized a crash was imminent, and they had time either to radio or to eject, they would have done so, "guilty" of pilot error or not.*]

e. There were no radio reports indicating any malfunction in any of Raider 58's systems between the time that the transponder was deactivated at 0903 and the last radio transmission at approximately 0922.
[*It is believed by some experts that the plane crashed within 1-2 minutes following the last radio transmission. Appendix 3.*]

f. The mountain peaks and ridges in the area of the mishap on the morning in question were obscured by clouds.
[*Not according to the photograph of Kavanaugh Ridge taken after the mishap by the witness, attorney Richard Brown, who was not wearing*

his watch at the time. Weather reports of the area for the hours closest to the mishap were not utilized. See Appendix 1 and 3.]

g. The last radio transmission from Raider 58 indicated that the mishap pilots were looking for clear weather below the clouds to enable them to complete the low-level navigational mission for which they had been scheduled.

["*Looking for clear weather" would never comprise a valid reason to descend precipitously far below the lowest peaks. See Appendix 3.*]

"Those facts lead to one conclusion: the mishap pilots intentionally descended into instrument meteorological conditions or marginal visual meteorological conditions and while attempting to do so impacted the ground in controlled flight. Under the known circumstances, that constitutes pilot error."

* * * * *

Although the investigative team contended it knew neither the location nor the cause of the crash during the 13 months the plane was missing, yet during that time the Navy insisted that *pilot error*—not malfunction—was the cause. "With the absence of the MSDRS and mission computers which were not salvaged from the debris, *it would be presumptuous* to reach factual conclusions," the commander wrote. He's absolutely correct, of course. The cause cannot be confirmed. But then he added, "The most probable cause factor can be attributed to *pilot error*."

To assume "pilot error" as "probable cause" based on the examination of engine components smashed to small pieces, and on the *absence* of the MSDRS and mission computers which were not recovered from the crash site, was conjectural at best and irresponsible at worst. Likewise was ignoring the auditory witness, failing to interview the other pilots immediately and omitting in the official JAG report the conflicting statement of a pilot in closest contact with Raider 58 during the time of the mishap. Conversations among pilots and precise times of interchange and activity are not recorded, so all witness responses were based on memory and conjecture after a two-week hiatus before interviews.

Accidents generally fit into one of four categories: *acts of nature*, such as lightning, birds, wind shear, weather; *malfunction*, such as equipment, mechanical, technical, or maintenance failure, including design or function; *physical problems*, such as heart attack, vertigo, fatigue; and finally, *pilot error*. Not much can be done about the first. The second is difficult to prove. The third is generally not identified in time, or is ignored. It implies that the pilot really did not have *the right stuff* after all. This sometimes overlaps the fourth and final cause of mishaps: pilot error. That is the catch-all, simple and clean—unless survivors start digging.

*****

One section of the Admiral's letter mandated further research. Why had Mike and Dan "violated" the MSL altitude rule of 18,000 feet? What does that action say about pilots who do so? Is violating the altitude rule analogous to exceeding the speed limit by a few miles on the highway within acceptable boundaries? Is it practiced regularly and without consequence or guilt by most pilots? Two military fighter-jet pilots explained: A *violation* does go on the record and connotes a far more serious breach of rules than does a *deviation*. Set limits are especially important when flying near other aircraft, as these four planes were. Each is assigned a safety zone with usually a thousand foot buffer between the routes. A deviation of 500 feet, however, is not considered unusual for short periods within the buffer zone.

CAPT Ginsberg had reported he was flying at 18,500; COL Kamp reported he was at 20,000 feet, which may or may not have been within Kamp's buffer zone. When a pilot slides into another zone, he is reminded either by a pilot in that vicinity whose radar indicates the altitude of planes in the area, or by the ATC.

Of course, Raider 58 clearly did not crash because it flew at 18,500 feet. It crashed because it plummeted 8,000 feet within minutes, far *below* any reasonable buffer in the Eastern Sierra.

APPENDIX 5

Jack Anderson

JACK ANDERSON and DALE VAN ATTA

Naval Aviator's Death a Mystery

Marilyn Ginsberg has been waiting for two years to bury her husband. Thanks to the secrecy of the U.S. Navy, she may never put to rest the mystery of his death.

Capt. Daniel Ginsberg was one of the Navy's esteemed "Top Guns." On May 20, 1987, his F18 jet crashed into the Sierra Nevada in California on a routine training flight. The Navy claimed it spent 1,388 flight hours searching for the wreckage. Then it gave up.

But Marilyn Ginsberg, with two toddlers, wouldn't give up. The more she read of the Navy's search records, the more hollow they sounded and she grew determined to find the plane herself.

A year after the accident she did, and it took only seven hours. Using the same information the Navy had, she had reward posters and maps hung in ranger stations, at trail heads and in sheriffs' offices. With reluctant help from the military, she initiated a search. Last June 18, after a half-day hike, a search team found the plane east of Yosemite National Park near the Nevada border.

Finding the plane so easily raised far more questions than it answered for Mrs. Ginsberg and the family of the dead copilot, Lt. Michael Mueller. Why hadn't the Navy spotted it? Was the Navy hiding something? Why would a pilot, respected for his caution, who had flown the 1986 bombing raid on Libya, crash on a routine flight across California?

The Pentagon has locked the records of the crash in a vault for top-secret material and will release only a sanitized version of its conclusions.

Our associate Jim Lynch pored over documents and interviewed more than a dozen people privy to the crash and the search. We found convincing evidence that the Navy may have known exactly where the plane was, and decided to leave it there.

The plane crashed on a ridge behind Green Creek Canyon. The Navy records show that no search aircraft were near the canyon on the day of the crash. Yet a hiker and a forestry worker swear they saw Navy planes fly in and out of the canyon hours after the crash. A deputy at a nearby sheriff's department saw a helicopter equipped to pick up wreckage a couple of days after the accident.

A hiker reported an "explosion" near the crash site and the last radar reading from the F18 was less than three miles from the crash site. But the Navy focused its search 30 miles away on Glass Mountain.

A Navy spokesman told us the official search was thorough and that the wreckage could not be seen from the air. But if the Navy found the plane, why was it kept a secret? It may have something to do with chronic mechanical problems in F18s, including sporadic engine fires.

Three more F18s crashed after Capt. Ginsberg's ill-fated flight. Officially, the Navy says an F18 fire has never killed anyone.

A top Navy official, who asked not to be identified, told us Capt. Ginsberg made a dumb mistake and dipped down out of the clouds for better visibility. That explanation bothers another F18 pilot who had flown with Ginsberg for more than 100 hours and said he was "real cautious."

The Navy is still identifying remains taken from the rubble. The Ginsbergs and the Muellers hope to have it all sorted out by May 20 so they can bury their men on the second anniversary of the crash.

From the *Washington Post*, Friday, April 14, 1989, E5:

Naval Aviator's Death a Mystery
By Jack Anderson and Dale Van Atta

Marilyn Ginsberg has been waiting for two years to bury her husband. Thanks to the secrecy of the U.S. Navy, she may never put to rest the mystery of his death.

Capt. Daniel Ginsberg was one of the Navy's esteemed "Top Guns." On May 20, 1987, his F18 jet crashed into the Sierra Nevada in California on a routine training flight. The Navy claimed it spent 1,388 flight hours searching for the wreckage. Then it gave up.

But Marilyn Ginsberg, with two toddlers, wouldn't give up. The more she read of the Navy's search records, the more hollow they sounded and she grew determined to find the plane herself.

A year after the accident she did, and it took only seven hours. Using the same information the Navy had, she had reward posters and maps hung in ranger stations, at trail heads and in sheriffs' offices. With reluctant help from the military, she initiated a search. Last June 18, after a half-day hike, a search team found the plane east of Yosemite National Park near the Nevada border.

Finding the plane so easily raised far more questions than it answered for Mrs. Ginsberg and the family of the dead copilot, Lt. Michael Mueller. Why hadn't the Navy spotted it? Was the Navy hiding something? Why would a pilot, respected for his caution, who had flown the 1986 bombing raid on Libya, crash on a routine flight across California?

The Pentagon has locked the records of the crash in a vault for top-secret material and will release only a sanitized version of its conclusions.

Our associate Jim Lynch pored over documents and interviewed more than a dozen people privy to the crash and the search. We found convincing evidence that the Navy may have known exactly where the plane was, and decided to leave it there.

The plane crashed on a ridge behind Green Creek Canyon. The Navy records show that no search aircraft were near the canyon on the day of the crash. Yet a hiker and a forestry worker swear they saw Navy planes fly in and out of the canyon hours after the crash. A deputy at a nearby sheriff's department saw a helicopter equipped to pick up wreckage a couple of days after the accident.

A hiker reported an "explosion" near the crash site and the last radar reading from the F18 was less than three miles from the crash site. But the Navy focused its search 30 miles away on Glass Mountain.

A Navy spokesman told us the official search was thorough and that the wreckage could not be seen from the air. But if the Navy found the plane, why was it kept a secret? It may have something to do with chronic mechanical problems in F18s, including sporadic engine fires.

Three more F18s crashed after Capt. Ginsberg's ill-fated flight. Officially, the Navy says an F18 fire has never killed anyone.

A top Navy official, who asked not to be identified, told us Capt. Ginsberg made a dumb mistake and dipped down out of the clouds for better visibility. That explanation bothers another F18 pilot who had flown with Ginsberg for more than 100 hours and said he was "real cautious."

The Navy is still identifying remains taken from the rubble. The Ginsbergs and the Muellers hope to have it all sorted out by May 20 so they can bury their men on the second anniversary of the crash.

APPENDIX 6

Investigating Military Mishaps

Numerous mishap widows understand both Marilyn's feelings and her questions. Even with little or no recourse, many military families involved in such battles refuse to give up until learning the real reasons for a loved one's death. Pilots themselves maintain a critical interest in discovering reasons for aircraft accidents in the military. After all, they say, it's their skin at risk. But because the military is its "own judge and jury," the cause of fatal accidents is often conveniently ascribed to the victim.

Journalist Steve Johnson reported extensive research on such accidents in a series of four articles appearing in the San Jose *Mercury News Report* (Monday, July 17, 1989). More than one thousand men and women die each year in U.S. military *peacetime* accidents. He cited examples to show that the cause of death often attaches blame either to the victim or to the circumstances, such as a medical condition, rather than to the primary reason for the mishap. He included the following:

Daniel Ginsberg and Michael Mueller flew an F-18 into the Sierra Nevada at 10,400 feet after a quick descent from 18,500 feet. *Cause: pilot error.*

Ted Harduvel steered his F-16 into the ground in Korea. He had told his wife if he ever went down, "Get yourself a copy of the safety report and the best attorney in town, because it ain't going to be my fault." *Cause: pilot error.*

Michael Bowden suffocated when the air-valve failed on his protective suit. His mother had begged politicians and military officials to release her only child from the Alameda-based USS Enterprise because he had suffered a seizure the year before, had dizzy spells, and nearly fainted several times on board. He was to have been observed on a television monitor, but it was pointed in the wrong direction. When he lost consciousness, a medical team was delayed in reaching him for another 5-8 minutes. *Cause: heart attack.*

James Friend III collapsed and died during a forced run at boot camp after already collapsing several times during that routine. He had been diagnosed with sickle-cell trait, which some research indicates a risk of sudden death during rigorous exercise. *Cause: Sickle-cell trait.*

John Jordan and Wesley Dean felt their F-2D Phantom fighter

stall above the Arizona desert and plunge into a steep dive. They attempted to eject; the plane exploded on impact. Dean was said to have falsified flying records to "exaggerate abilities and qualify for flight pay." A memo to crew members followed: "If you're going to lie, then be smart at least." *Cause: Pilot error.*

Michael Daniel crashed while wearing regulation goggles that supposedly allow military helicopter pilots to see better at night. Two weeks earlier, a confidential memorandum from an official stated that the goggles had "resulted in tragic and unnecessary deaths—134 of them." One day before the crash, Daniel reported he couldn't see while wearing them. *Cause: Pilot error.*

Ross Mulhare crashed his Stealth jet into the California desert, having been noticeably fatigued before the flight. A memo written less than 24 hours earlier from an Air Force official stated that test pilots were often too exhausted to fly safely. He likened the flying schedule to a "time bomb." "I believe we are on a collision course with a mishap." *Cause: Pilot error.*

In the painfully tedious and often unsuccessful attempt to find out what really caused these deaths, the journalist showed their reasons for believing that cover-up is routine and protected. The military keeps two sets of books on accidents: the whitewashed one for public consumption and the private report that provides such data as safety records, recommendations, and any implication of equipment failure or bureaucracy error.

It is widely accepted that the military and the manufacturers of military hardware "investigate themselves." Part of their protection derives from a 1950 Supreme Court ruling (the Feres doctrine) that bars lawsuits against military personnel, with few exceptions, even if gross negligence is the cause. Another Supreme Court ruling, passed after Mike and Dan went down, provides immunity to defense contractors, with the stipulation that the manufacturers who sell such equipment not only obtain approval of designs from the military, but also warn the Pentagon of potential dangers.

But Supreme Court Justice William Brennan suggested in the case of David Boyle, whose accidental death in 1983 was blamed on a manufacturer, that "any law absolving multibillion-dollar private enterprises from answering for their tragic mistakes is troubling." Some would call it diabolical. Referring to the Boyle decision, Johnson noted: "Companies can avoid liability for defective equipment if the military approved reasonably precise specifications for the product. But, the god-like military officials often lack technical expertise to spot inherent dangers in those specifications." Dave Hall, an independent accident reviewer and former Navy safety official, suggested that if a dishonest contractor doesn't mention that its product has a dangerous design flaw, how would the military know? Furthermore, why would the military ever approve a product with a known flaw?

Some, including many military officials, do not agree with the dual system. For example, Johnson pointed out that the National Transportation Safety Board, which investigates everything from civilian plane crashes to train wrecks, makes all records public. NTSB officials say that openness has helped—not hurt—their ability to investigate accidents, and that it is *essential to the agency's credibility.*

Francis McGlade, the Army's director of safety for ten years, said that "the Pentagon has permitted a large number of needless deaths and injuries . . . and gives safety low priority. The safety function carries no weight. We would crank that into the budget cycle to fix [something], and it always came out at the bottom of the priority list. So, it would never get fixed."

Major Bill Cunningham who oversees legal matters for the Army Safety Center, on the other hand, agrees with many DOD officials that their safety measures are working. He pointed to a decline [from more than 1500 in 1980 to less than 1100 in 1988] in fatal military accidents in the last decade. "That makes everybody around here feel pretty good," he said.

To believe that anyone in the military wants to lose personnel in accidents is preposterous. No one suggests that the DOD and all branches of the U.S. Armed Services do not advocate improved safety for all. But even while defending the overall safety record, Captain Vince Huth, director of aviation safety programs at the Naval Postgraduate School in Monterey, conceded that change moves slowly. "The speed at which safety recommendations get [action] is sometimes very frustrating," he acknowledged. Huth himself has urged changes, including strengthening the power of safety officials. In an article he wrote for a Navy publication in 1988, Huth noted: "The staggering human and material cost indicates we can and must improve our safety performance."

Johnson related this incident: After an attorney at the Justice Department discovered a contractor's defective part had contributed to the cause of a fatal crash, he proposed legal action against the company, but the Pentagon rejected the idea: "We can't do that. We can't be suing our own contractors."

Despite the jury's guilty verdict (overturned in the Boyle case) and numerous other fatal crashes involving Sikorsky helicopters, company spokesperson Marty Moore knew of no instances in which the military had fined or otherwise disciplined the manufacturer. In fact, officials at the Army and Air Force safety centers were unable to provide a single example of punitive measures against a violation by a company directly responsible for safety.

APPENDIX 7

RE: Recommendations, Requests, Results

In a letter to Admiral __________ on 9 August 1993, I wrote:

Commander, Naval Safety Center
Naval Air Station
375 A Street
Norfolk, VA 23511

Dear Admiral __________:

Having been referred to you by the Deputy Assistant Judge Advocate General for investigations, Commander __________ in the Alexandria office, I seek information from the MIR regarding the F/A-18 aircraft mishap that occurred on May 20, 1987, resulting in the deaths of Marine Captain Daniel J. Ginsberg and First Lieutenant Michael D. Mueller.

I am currently writing the epilogue to a biography of LT Mueller. The requested information could alleviate lingering pain for the pilots' families if affirmative answers indicate that safety and survival have increased as a result of learning through this and other mishaps.

First, were the following two recommendations implemented?

1. an *impact-activated Emergency Locator Transmitter* for the F/A-18
2. an *impact-resistant, brightly colored MSDRS,* or similar flight recorder for the F/A-18 and other tactical aircraft

Second, were the following two changes implemented?

1. GE agreed to replace the F-404 engines after about 250 of the fleet of 384 F-18's were grounded due to titanium engine fires associated with the break-up of engine compressor blades
2. The Navy decided to apply a fire-resistant coating to the engines.

Finally, in the investigation reports concerning this mishap, which were sent to the families, portions were redacted, and in some of the blank spaces were these handwritten notations: *None of your business.* Although such an insult would not be sanctioned by the military community, the very absence of information after repeated requests for it is in itself offensive. Copied samples of these pages are enclosed.

The families and I are aware of typical reasons given for the redactions (classified military tactics, operational missions, classified equipment/technology, protection of witnesses, safety of the pilots, national security, etc.) but through the FOIPA, I request either the non-redacted portions or an explanation for each and every redaction.

I truly appreciate your response to these questions. The families and I want to relinquish both our questions and our pain after more than six years.

Sincerely,

Martha E. Chamberlain

In response to the notations, "None of your business," I received this reply:

Regarding " . . . inappropriate comments found on copies of the MIR obtained by the families of the deceased, please be assured these comments did not originate from documents released by the Naval Safety Center. I am as distressed by these comments as you are. However, the MIR concerning this accident was provided to several requesters and what happens to the MIR after release is out of our control." [Although the notations were not acknowledged or endorsed by military officials, the documents *were sent* to the families by the military office.]

In response to letters sent to a variety of military personnel to whom I was referred with the above questions, I received in July 1994 the following information, with drawings, that confirm implementation of the recommendations by the investigators. The anticipated increase in the margin of safety and survival for other F/A-18 pilots in some sense alleviates the pain and loss for family and friends.

From the Naval Air Systems Command:

1. "A deployable flight incident recorder system (DFIRS) was developed for installation in F/A-18-C/D aircraft. Provisions for installation of DFIRS were incorporated into Block 35 Lot 14 aircraft starting in September 1991. Complete installation . . . commenced with Block 40 Lot 15 aircraft starting in June 1993. Retrofit of Block 35 to 39 aircraft with DFIRS is planned in the near future.

"The DFIRS is designed to survive aircraft mishaps and record the last 30 minutes [rather than 15 seconds] of flight data prior to the incident. An emergency locator transmitter is integral to the DFIRS System.

2. "The DFIRS is bright orange in color [thereby facilitating location] and will record the last 30 minutes of flight data as previously stated. There is a mission need statement for all tactical aircraft to carry the DFIRS." [Only the cover plate of the MSDRS for Raider 58 was located. Grey in color, it blended with most of the aircraft and the landscape.]

3. Regarding the F-404 engines: "First and third stage compressor blades have been redesigned and a fire-resistant coating has been implemented for the outer bypass duct of the engine.

"[Furthermore], the DFIRS is employed under any of these conditions: 1) aircrew ejection 2) aircraft crash 3) aircraft submersion under water."

In response to the multiple requests for more than six years by the families and me, within the FOIPA, for the non-redacted portions or an explanation for those omissions supported by law, I received the same negative answers and the same reasons for not complying.

In response to multiple requests by the families and me for the pathology reports on the remains, the Muellers received their first written report from the AFIP in 1993.

APPENDIX 8

Bibliography
(Included are only a sampling of a vast number of articles about military mishaps.)

Anderson, Jack and Dale Van Atta. "Naval Aviator's Death a Mystery." *The Washington Post,* April 14, 1989, E5.

Associated Press. "F-14 Crashes; All Grounded." *Richmond Times Dispatch,* Feb. 23, 1996, A1,7.

Aviation Week.

"Critics Fault U.S. Army Helicopter Training with Night Vision Goggles." Mar. 27, 1989.

"Damaged C-130 Lands Safely in Alaska." Feb. 3, 1992, 15.

"A Kentucky." Feb. 10, 1992, 14.

"U.S. Air Force U-2 Crashed." Jan. 20, 1992, 17.

Cockburn, A. "Beat the Devil: Great Balls of Fire. *Nation.* July 23, 1988, 44.

Francke, Linda Bird. "The Aftershocks of a Woman Pilot's Death." *Glamour,* June 1995, 87.

Johnson, Steve. *Mercury News,* Series: July 16, 17, 18, 1989.

"Casualties of Neglect: Accidents in the Military."

"Counseling Comes Up Short."

"Deadly Secrets in the Service."

"Funeral Is Free; So Are Flag, Lapel Pins."

"How to Make Military Toe a New Line."

"Justice Not Swift Or Sure."

"Official Blunders Add Insult to Reality for Victims' Families."

"Shroud of Secrecy Covers Details of Deaths."

"Tales of Fervor and Fear: How Four Died."

"Widows Get Marching Orders: 90 Days to Move Out."

Mann, Paul. "Crash Query." *Aviation Week,* June 5, 1995, 21.

News for You. "A.F. Charges Six in Helicopter Tragedy." *News for You,* Sept. 21, 1994.

Maclean's. "CF-18 Pilot Dies." *Maclean's,* July 17, 1995, 95.

Moore, Molly. "Engine Problems Ground 250 Fighter Jets." *The Washington Post,* Nov. 21, 1987, A8.

Neuberger, Christine. "Pilot Seeks to Clear Navy Flier." *Times Dispatch,* Aug. 7, 1994.

Schmitt, Eric. "Military Works to Reduce Its Risks." *Richmond Times Dispatch*, Dec. 28, 1995.

Simpson, Sandra L. "Military MIRs and You." *Flying*, January 1995, 38-41.

Thompson, Mark. "Way, Way Off in the Wild Blue Yonder." *Time*, May 29, 1995, 32-33.

Thompson, Mark. "So, Who's to Blame?" *Time*, July 3, 1995, 27.

Time. "Bermuda Triangle: It's Still the Lost Squadron." *Time*, June 17, 1991, 32.

Underwood, Anne and Melinda Beck. "Unsolved Mystery." *Newsweek*, Sept. 11, 1995, 48-52.

U.S. News and World Report. "Hultgreen, Kara." *U.S. News and World Report*, Mar. 13, 1995, 16.

Wilkinson, Stephan. "After the Dust Settles." *Air and Space Smithsonian*, Apr./May, 1995, 10.

APPENDIX 9

Publicity Poster Offering Reward

MISSING AIRCRAFT

$5000 REWARD

The families of Captain Daniel Ginsberg, USMC, and First Lieutenant Michael Mueller, USMC, have authorized a reward of $5,000 for information leading to the discovery of the crash site of the FA-18 Hornet they were flying. The two pilots and their aircraft disappeared in the Sierra Nevada mountains on May 20, 1987.

The reward offer expires December 31, 1988.

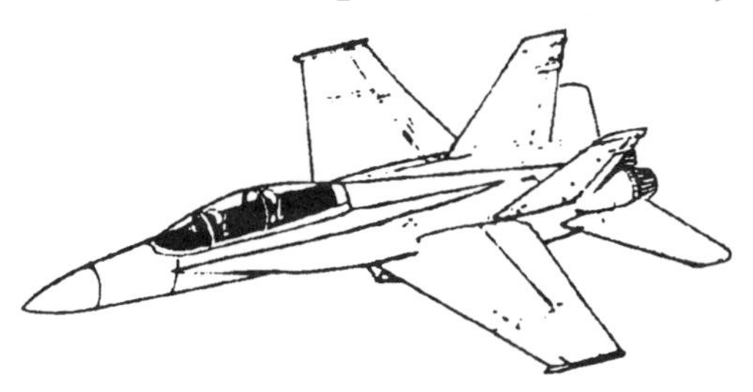

The FA-18 Hornet strikefighter from Naval Air Station (NAS) Lemoore, California, was lost while on a training flight from NAS Lemoore to NAS Fallon, Nevada. The last known position of the aircraft was in the Hoover Wilderness area, southwest of Bridgeport near Twin Lakes. Their intended flight path would have taken them north from that point. To date the aircraft has not been found. The parents, wives and children of the missing pilots would like to locate their loved ones for obvious reasons. Please spread the word to other people you know who go to the mountains. Your interest and assistance in this matter is greatly appreciated.

If you notice any of the following, please report it to your nearest Forest Ranger, or call collect (209) 998-3183

- **Aircraft wreckage**
- **Unexplained metal, gray or black in color**
- **Unexplained burned spots or blackened earth**
- **Tree tops sheared for no apparent reason**

Aircraft wreckage with an "X" painted on it are previously discovered wrecks. If portions of an aircraft are found, please do not touch anything. Although the jet carried no ordnance, the ejection seats contain explosives, and pressurized containers may explode. Please just note its location and report it.

APPENDIX 10

Mike's Essay: 6E504 SOLO

The morning was a crisp 32 and clear as crystal. At 0600 I walked into "East Line Brief." Even at that early hour my heart was pounding as I stepped up to the flight duty officer, Lt. Lee, with my request. "Do you have any solo planes today?" In my heart I already knew the answer . . . airplane availability had been 25 percent at best.

"Sure do, Lieutenant." His answer shocked me . . . With the intense pleasure of a student pilot ready for his solo debut, I copied my event and side number, 6E504 SOLO and walked on the air that had become my friend toward "my" aircraft. Even if my flying skills were about to be scrutinized, I didn't care. I was ready. I was in command of a T-34C turbo-mentor . . . it is nothing to scoff at . . . fully aerobatic, capable of making one give up his lunch. With sheer disbelief I found myself leaning into the rear cockpit, securing it for solo flight. As I strapped into my parachute and harness I thought, They are letting me—no, they are requiring me—no, even better, they are paying me to take this finely tuned, high-performance machine to break the bonds of earth's grasp and soar with the eagles . . .

With checklists complete, I was ready to start. No one was in back to take charge this time if something went wrong; it was only me—and God. But that was why I had been working so hard these last few months. Not only was this my first solo, but also exactly one year ago I had graduated from TBS . . .

A good start in 30 seconds! A call for taxi and I was rolling for the runup area. Waiting for clearance, I had a few minutes to relish God's presence and the beauty of the morning's golden sunshine exploding around me. "They that wait upon the Lord shall renew their strength; they shall mount up with wings as eagles; they shall run and not be weary; they shall walk, and not faint (Is. 40:31 KJV). I was ready to "mount up." God was my strength.

"6E504, cleared for takeoff, Number 1," the controller's voice interrupted the calm. I taxied into position . . . and I was on the roll . . . with a normal takeoff, departure and climbout, I was on my way to the working area 1 at 170 knots, dazzled by the sight below me: plush, chartreuse fields, the contrasting deep, dark green forest, and the sparkling peninsula bay basking in brilliant morning sun.

What a perfect day for the first solo! With Saufley Field beckoning me to a touch-and-go landing, the only requirement on this flight prior to returning to NAS Whiting Field, I called for their instructions . . . And I pulled power to commence my first solo "break."

No instructor in the back to tell me to stay on airspeed and altitude, and to pick up the correct wingtip distance, which, of course, I was struggling to do anyway. No, none of that. Just me, telling myself to perform as I had learned.

After the sixth touch-and-go, all of which were well done, but with no one in the back seat to acknowledge it, I radioed a quick call, "Number 1 upwind, departing." Now it was time to play! At 800 feet above ground at 170 knots, five miles from airport traffic, I was at max-power, 15 degree nose-up, a perfect place to begin.

Leveling off at 8500 feet at fast cruise found me heading to Secour Bay . . . First, I had to go fast. For the same reason grown men drive ultra-expensive cars at ridiculous speeds in big circles on a race track, I felt the exhilarating fascination human beings have with high speed. 280 knots is the limit, so I was conservative at 275 knots; I wouldn't have wanted to get in trouble on the first solo or have the plane disintegrate. Not only would that have cut my solo short and ruined my whole day, but one does not want to make a "silk-descent" on his first solo!

Then a few tight turns to squeeze me into my seat to take full advantage of that machine, all the while absorbing the thrill of the awesomeness of the moment. A smooth, level pull-out and I was a fast cruise . . . I had only 35 minutes remaining before my airplane would turn into a pumpkin, and 60 miles to return to home plate.

A magnificent morning, sent just for me from my Father above. An enjoyable entry on "course rules." Homefield break, yes, a little overshoot on the final roll out, but a good recovery . . . Once again I was clenched tightly by earth's strong grasp. But I had been free for a time, and I would be again, God willing . . .

APPENDIX 11

Mike's Essay: Landing on the LEX

"Cintra 001, your signal is Charlie" . . . Four TA-4J Skyhawks were ready to board the U.S.S. Lexington off the Florida Keys . . . Always fascinated with flying and with aircraft carriers, now I was about to qualify in a tactical jet aboard a carrier as one of the final phases before being "winged" as a Naval Aviator in the Marine Corps.

Excitement and tension gave way to procedures and checklists as the "Lex" grew larger. I would soon land a seven-ton jet on something that looked like I could play with in the bath tub.

The objective is to hold a precise attitude on the aircraft . . . The pilot sees a "meatball" and makes continuous corrections to keep it in the center all the way to touchdown . . . Glidescope must be maintained with a few feet to ensure landing within the eighty-foot strip where the tailhook can engage an arresting wire . . .

As I barrelled down the shoot at 130 knots, approximately 143 miles per hour, my left hand was making an infinite number of small throttle movements. I reacted to minute ball changes and anticipated its movement by feeling the aircraft move with the sensitive instrument on board . . . my seat. Meatball, line-up, angle of attack, meatball, line-up meatball, meatball, meatball. Without notice the Skyhawk slammed down onto the deck. Max power and aft stick lifted me back into the air . . .

Everything was happening fast . . . With checklist complete I turned downwind to get up for my first "trap" in the TA-4J. I was getting more relaxed and confident as I rolled into the groove, eager for my first arrestment. Meatball, meatball, meatball, slam, max power . . . there was no jerk. An aft tug on the stick and I was flying again. The hook had jumped over the number three and number four wire, so I got to make three touch-and-goes that lovely day.

The next six passes I snagged a wire each time, some "prettier" than others, but got aboard. An arrested landing is close to indescribable. It is an awesome sensation to be going 130 knots one moment and the next moment slamming down, jerking and lurching forward in the seat, being held clear of the instrument panel only by the harness, which you hope was locked before landing. All of this occurs in approximately 100 feet. Some say that it is like driving a car into a brick wall at 145 miles per hour, but I have yet to do that so I cannot say for sure . . .

As if that was not enough excitement for one day, now I had to get back in the air, going from 0 to 130 in 200 feet . . . The aircraft is hooked to the catapult, goes to max power, a button is pushed and away it goes. . . The pilot is slammed back into the seat . . . the aircraft is going off the front of the ship whether the pilot stands on the brakes, shuts the engine down, or decides he really does not want to go on this ride.

After six such traps and cats, the carrier evolution is over, for now.

"450, steer 160 degrees . . . you're a qual [carrier qualified]."

What bliss those words brought . . . I had completed the most challenging stage in the advanced strike aircraft syllabus. As I streaked the sixty miles back to Key West, the sun bouncing off the magnificent aqua-blue water [reflected] my elation! I prayed and thanked God for His protection, for . . . carrier qualification, and most of all, for God's filling my life with the joy that only He can give.

APPENDIX 12

The Single Man's Search for a Righteous Fox

right with God
manifests fruits of the Spirit
professional mom
conservative
believes in inerrancy of the Word
active in Bible studies and ministries
generous
has personal devotions
memorizes Scripture
disciplined and discipling
no gossip
full of prayer
actively seeking to share her faith
corresponds with friends/relatives
proper use of English language
athletic
trim—NFC [no fat chicks]
reads kids Bible stories a lot
public modesty
120 lb. max (according to height)
smiles a lot
clean and well-groomed
attractive now and later
loves outdoor activities
optimistic
encouraging
speech and silence
no favoritism
hates cats
musical
respectable
conservative Republican
loves children (but not for awhile)
always available to the kids
sociable/likes to entertain
no public criticism of me
supportive of me
max-communicable
no moodiness
example of Christian growth
Proverbs 31—an example of
feminine
ladylike
likes Christian music
serious about GT's [good times]
constructively challenges/encourages
self/others to maximize potential
5' to 5'9"
stays in shape
dependent/independent
ability to teach others
versatile in roles
laughs/makes others laugh
courteous to all/friendly
no heavy makeup
stylish, not faddish
First Aid/medically inclined
perfectionist/realist
motivated and a motivator
anti-TV
productive time management
doesn't waste time

admirable
romantic
back rubs
very neat/clean/orderly house
cook
frugal/financial wizard
submissive/determined
follows/leads well; managerial capabilities
bright and intelligent
college-educated
common sense
healthy attitude toward sex
hard physical worker
healthy self-image
likes to learn new things; anti-rut
individual goals/aspirations
plans to achieve realistically
level-headed under pressure
discrete in displaying affection
homemaker
appreciates the arts
sincere belief she can make
herself/the world better
sincere
purposeful
humble
diligent/not lazy
not afraid to sweat
enjoys a challenge
open-minded

APPENDIX 13

Acronyms/Abbreviations/Terms

AA	Aviation Administration
AASF	Army Aviation Support Facility
ADM	Admiral
AFIP	Armed Forces Institute of Pathology
AI	Aviation Indoctrination
ARRC	Aerospace Rescue and Recovery Center
ATC	Air Traffic Control
BAMRU	Bay Area Mountain Rescue Unit
CACO	Casualty Assistance Commanding Officer
CAP	Civil Air Patrol
CAPT	Captain
Carrier	a Navy ship that launches and recovers aircraft
CAT	shots slang for catapult launch from carriers
CAVU	Clear and Visibility Unobstructed
CDR	Commander
CO	Commanding Officer
COL	Colonel
COMNAVAIRPAC	Commander Naval Aviation Pacific Command
DFIRS	Deployable Flight Incident Recorder System
DIS	Defense Investigative Service
DNA	Deoxyribonucleic acid "fingerprinting" used for indentification
DOD	Department of Defense
earth resources palette	a means to detect an object in a body of water through an electro-magnetic frequency band
EI	Engineering Investigation
FAA	Federal Aviation Administration
FLIR	Forward Looking Infra-Red; weather

	information displayed on screen
flying the meatball:	a method used on approach for landing on a carrier, by watching a system of lights to gauge a precise attitude, altitude and azimuth (compass heading)
FNAV-173	a training flight in the syllabus
G-suit	anti-gravity suit worn to counteract pooling of blood in extremities
HUD	Heads Up Display; the primary flight instrument
Hughes APG radar	used for navigation and attack information
IFF	Identification Friend or Foe; enhances image on radar screen
IFR	Instrument Flight Rules
IP	Instructor Pilot
IUT	Instructor Under Training
JAG	Judge Advocate General (an attorney for the Navy)
knot	a division of the log's line that equals one nautical mile
LKP	Last Known Position
LT	Lieutenant
MA	Mishap Aircraft
MAD	Magnetic Anomaly Detection; used to locate missing aircraft
MAJ	Major
MCMWTC	Marine Corps Mountain Warfare Training Center
MIA/POW	persons designated as Missing In Action or Prisoner of War
MIR	Mishap Investigative Report
MSDRS	Maintenance Signal Data Recorder System; flight recorder
NAS	Naval Air Station

NASA	National Aeronautics and Space Agency
NM	Nautical Mile; unit of distance used in navigation in sea or air based on the earth's curvature; equals about 6076 feet
NWCAP	Nevada Wing CAP
PAX	Patuxent River NAS
Plebe	first-year student in military or naval academy
radar skin painting	a slang term referring to the ability to be tracked by radar
Raider	the call sign for designated aircraft in Mike's squadron
RP	Replacement Pilot (in training to replace those who have completed course)
SAR	Search and Rescue
squawk	a slang term meaning to initiate a radar signal on the IFF
tailhook	a device on the plane that snags a wire on the jet to facilitate stopping when a jet lands on a carrier
TBS	The Basic School: for training Marine officers, Quantico, Virginia
USGS	United States Geological Survey
USMC	United States Marine Corps
USNA	United States Naval Academy
VFA-125	Mike's squadron
VFR	Visual Flight Rules
VMC	Visual Meteorlogical Conditions, referring to weather conditions
WX	Weather
XO	Executive Officer

ABOUT THE AUTHOR

Martha Gunsalus Chamberlain received the Silver Angel Award from Religion in Media (1989) for her first book, *Surviving Junior High* (Herald Press). She co-authored *Hymn Devotions for All Seasons* (1989, Abingdon Press). Her third book, *The Ultimate Flight* (1996, The Word Press) is in its second printing (Wesley Press, 1997). Her devotional themes and articles have been published in *1992 Disciplines* (The Upper Room), *A Calendar of Devotions* (1989, Abingdon Press), *Partnership, Wesleyan Woman, New World Outlook, Discipleship Journal, Woman's Touch* and others.

Married to Bishop Ray W. Chamberlain for 37 years, Martha has three children, a daughter-in-law, two grandsons, and a foster daughter and her family. Following four years as a missionary nurse in Zambia, she continued nursing until led to new opportunities in writing, editing and teaching (Beginning Writers WordShops*). Currently living in Knoxville, Tennessee, she continues to write and to lead others to tell their story.

[*The spelling is correct as given: *WordShops*]